A Bagful of Kittens Headed to the Lake

*Selected Essays
by Cathy Carlton Hews*

Published in December 2019

A BAGFUL OF KITTENS HEADED TO THE LAKE © 2019

For My Father

The House

Dad had built the rock wall in the yard. I remember that. He added on a porch. He tended the flower garden, built a swing on the lawn. I vaguely remember those things happening. I was out at 19, long gone, real gone. If/when home improvements happened while I was living here, I don't remember/blocked. He was a long haul truck driver, later a milk truck operator, gone for long stretches (who wouldn't be, wouldn't you?). He did what he could with the house, when he could.

I walk in and put the cat carrier down, let Denny out. Dena follows me with boxes; she empties the car of the rest of my meager satchels of crap. Please don't let her look around at this house, please let her just stare straight ahead, not seeing anything. I don't come from here, I never lived here, this is not me, I can't be from here. She looks around. She walks up to Dad, says something nice to him, he nods, understanding somewhat that I am moving back (not to take care of him, he doesn't understand that yet, I think I made up some load of shit about that as to not alarm him, and to allow me time for a sit-rep). She comes back to me. Oh, Betty, those blue eyes are just like yours. Yeah, yeah, I say… Thanks Dena, just get back on the road, you can't stay here longer, you can't witness my horror and shame and life-crash any more, don't want lunch, don't have to go to the bathroom.

Betty, I have to go to the bathroom.

The bathroom ceiling is coming down. A single bulb hangs. The wall is peeling off around the tub. The tub is rusted, cobwebby (I had been told by the State of Massachusetts that he hadn't been washing changing).

Elsewhere, the fluorescent lights that my parents had hung were blinking, some working, some not. The ceilings were water damaged, cracked, plaster falling off. The floor was coming up in his bedroom; the door leading to the porch off the room was swollen shut. Piss wafted from the floorboards. His bed (a fucking fucking

8

waterbed my brother had talked him into in the '80's) was somehow neatly all made up with shitty sheets that Dad never noticed.

Dena comes out of the bathroom. I stand in the kitchen, in shock. She kindly murmurs something about hating to have to leave me. I think I nodded and mumbled something back, in shock. I watch her drive away.

Hey Dad, we will work on fixing some stuff up around here, what do you think? We have some work to do on the house.
He looks blankly at me, and asks why, what's wrong with the house?

I shuffle to the kitchen and put down food for the cat. Dennis, though, has disappeared, not to be found for three days. Who can blame him? Tempting to join him, squeezed, twisted, twirled into a furry pile somewhere in the recesses of Hellshack. (Later, I started to blog, and the Hellshack moniker stuck.)

Hey Dad, let's go out to dinner tonight. Tomorrow I will unpack and shop, but tonight, you and I can go out for a beer.

A Room Full of Crap

Chirrup, chirrup... Nonstop now for two days. Where the fuck is that fucking cricket in this hellhole? There is so much crap in this room I can barely kick my way through it, and now a hidden, chirruping, non-stopping, Godless cricket has taken up happy residence? I will go madder than Lucia di Lammermoor if I don't lay my RAID-wielding paws on it. A cricket in the house is good luck? Did I read that somewhere? Is it a sin to kill a mockingbird, or a cricket?

I'll never be able to find it in this room (chirrup). Ever since moving back here several months ago, I have been unable to wade through the flotsam of thirty years of neglect. It was all I could do to plunk down the laptop, unzip the cat carrier, dump out a pile of panties from one of the Hefties, and get to it. Make doctor appointments, coordinate (chirrup) meds, find decent elder care services, talk him into wearing Depends. They cost HOW much?

Nope, not happening to me. Keep pretending I live in New York or LA, not back here in this hell shack in the woods. Walk around each pile of God Knows What. Don't even look at it, don't want to see old piles of photo albums, whatever videos she had, what stupid crazy books she collected. Broken, dusty chairs, cobwebby piles of unidentified junk. No, I do not want to sort through this crap. My only concession was putting that poster of Grand Central, you know, (chirrup) the one with the sun streaming through all the windows onto that beautiful concourse, at the foot of the ratty cot with the ratty window shade.

Nope, not happening to me. Bella, our health aide who comes and helps with him, pokes her head in. Do you want me to put him in the (chirrup) shower today?

Do you hear that fucking thing? She does. Inside the room? Yes, it sounds like it.

God, I have to put a hazmat suit on to move these piles of crap to even look for it. Yes, you might. Yes, thanks, Bella, I think he does need to go into the shower today.

I look over at the Widow Dennis perched on a windowsill, licking, grooming. Good luck, bub, getting the dust out of your fur. I, myself, have been lapping my arms for three months with no luck. And by the way, isn't it your Sacred Pussy Duty to at least keep me free from mice, wasps, and the fucking crickets that are driving Mommy insane? Yes, I have turned into that bat whose cat calls her Mommy. Shoot me now? Perhaps a little later? OK, up to you. What else would be the point of having a friggin cat here in the country? The Widow, nonplussed, looks up, blinks a few times and returns to lapping.

I hear the shower discussion in the next room. Bella has convinced him that it is a pretty good idea and I hear them make their slow way to the bathroom.

I get up and kick one of the piles of crap.

Chirrup.

Let's Play Said: Unsaid

The (long-haired) Widow had poop on his tail, as he is wont to have every now and again. Removal process entails flopping him upside down, legs a-floppin' and yowls a-flyin' (but the cat was pretty calm) and attacking the task at hand with soapy towels and small scissors.

Said: (Old One)

Well, what are we going to do with the cat?

Said: (Me)

What?

Said: (Old One)

Well, we could take him to the vet.

Said: (Me)

What?

Said: (Old One)

The vet could put him down, you know, because of the shitting.

Said: (Me)

In a million years that will never happen, do we understand each

other? And you are never to say that to me again. We're clear,

right?

Unsaid:

Because of the shitting? Huh? If anybody goes, it ain't gonna be

that cat.

Said: (Agency A)

Well, we can't have laundry day on Wednesday because of billing

purposes.

You just can't change the day to whatever you want every week.

Said: (Me)

(Silence)

Unsaid:

Are you fucking kidding me? I've got an old man, sick and

incontinent and I can't gauge exactly when I will need the laundry done. You guys might maybe wanna get real with what the client

really needs and worry less about your billing purposes. Actually, I

did offer up a cleaned up version of the Unsaid, even as I weighed

taking Pops to the vet.

Said: (Loyal Friend)

So, what are you doing for Thanksgiving?

We are flying off to Exotic Locale because it's time for a break.

Said: (Me)

I don't really know yet. Have fun!

Unsaid:

Actually I was wondering if I could fit my head into the oven along

with a turkey.

Two birds with one stone, ya know.

Said: (Caller)

(*on voice mail*)

Hi! We saw your resume on Monster, and my manager here at XYZ

Insurance Company wanted me to be sure to bring you in as we have

exciting sales opportunities for you!

Said: (Me)

(on their voice mail)

Oh thanks, anyway, but I am not sure if I have enough experience

for insurance sales.

Unsaid:

Jesus Christ I would rather slit my wrists and lap up my own blood.

Said: (Mechanic)

So, you have about two more months before we need to deal with

those brakes.

Said: (Me)

Oh yes, I will mark the calendar for that, can't be too careful about

vehicle maintenance.

Unsaid:

So, I can ride this bitch and cross my fingers till August 2015, yes?

Said: (VA Ray)

(on a house visit here after months of working with me figuring

out Dad's benefits)

Thank you for your service, sir. Sign here (and here and here) and we can get some things in place for you. (*And then to me*) You call me next week and we will also set some time aside to look at your options as caregiver, as it can be a little stressful.

Said: (Me)

(*LOUDLY and OFTEN*)

Thank you VA Ray, WE LOVE YOU!!!

Unsaid:

Not a thing. Not a thing unsaid to VA Ray.

The Blue Turtle

The Widow Dennis has sadly passed, due to a respiratory illness caused by the mold and mildew in the house. Not two days went by before the Shack was overrun with mice. Down to the shelter I went and swooped up the newest family member. As the cat howled in his carrier I said I hear you, bub. You can't howl louder than me. So, it's the two of us, howling. I'll figure out the mold, don't worry. Let's go see Grandpa, Cheddar.

His back inside hind leg is not only a little, well, reddish, a few raised bumps, scrape-y looking, fur long gone. Now it is oozy, somewhat bloody. I hadn't wanted to look this afternoon. I had wanted to keep my fingers crossed, my head down. Oh yes, that expensive antibiotic shot surely is doing the trick. Maybe all those other (I lost track of how many) vet visits, cortisone shots in the past six months were just lead-ins to this magic cure.

Cheddar has taken to compulsively licking the inside of his hind legs, also some of his belly. This is way more than the normal grooming regimen, but a psycho type of over-grooming to where the cat has licked the fur completely away.

I look, gingerly. He is asleep, groggy enough to not put up much of a fuss as I raise legs, push fur aside. Please don't let it be worse. Yes, worse. One side worse than the other, but neither side pretty. I minister with paper towels, hydrogen peroxide. He is awake enough now to bat me away and move toward the window.

I turn my attention to the other one.

Dad, do you want me to find a movie, or do you want to stay with the news?

Oh, it doesn't matter, whatever is on. I just watch the boys play ball.

Cheddar sits at the window. I watch his gait, he doesn't seem to be limping. It doesn't seem to hurt. It looks like it should hurt like a motherfucker. He sits at the window. I think about applying

Bag Balm. The New Englander in me.

But I am not a New Englander anymore, though I am waylaid

here for a time. It's fall, I remember fall in New York City. I

remember what the air felt like, thank God that City swelter is gone.

I smell apples, we moved faster on the streets, the light faded earlier.

We hopped from work to theatres, bars, symphonies. A little chill in

the air, we grabbed sweaters.

Dad, dinner in a half hour. Here are your pills. Let me check

your blood sugar. It was high this morning, gave him an insulin

shot. (Quick side-note, that insulin-shot-giving is a major pain in the

fucking ass. A major pain in the fucking ass. Jesus H. Christ, the

fucking VA people totally fucked it when they took him off

whatever the fuck that diabetic med he was on before all this fucking

shot-giving. He had an episode while off it, hence all this fucking

shot-giving now. This fucking shot-giving totally fucks me now.

Totally fucks me. Before the fucking shot-giving I could leave him

with the aides for a day or two, leave his pills out, have to shop and

cook for a week to leave him meals, but it was DO-ABLE. The

aides aren't allowed to fucking shot-give, so I am pretty well nonstop stuck now. No Exit. And of course, all this before the foster care program, speaking of stuck, but that's another paragraph, page, ream. Are you good for a half hour? Chicken tonight, and I picked up some squash.

OK dear.

I decide against the Bag Balm for Cheddar. I worry about the open wound.

I talk to a friend in Los Angeles. Life, the theatre. I wonder if I should get new headshots. I can't get them done here. Fuck.

Cheddar wants to be outside, that's really the problem. It's not the food, he doesn't have fleas. This self-mutilation of his started a couple of months after he moved in with us. He would start to cry at the door and windows. He darted for the door every time it opened. He clawed at screen windows. Other OCD-ish behavior occurred. He chewed every paper in sight. He would raid the pens, carrying pens off to unknown recesses beneath beds. He would whisk away little totems I had on my desk. I had three little bobble-head turtles I kept as group. It comforted me to see them together. I would arrange them so they would all lean in on each other, bobbing together. I was unusually upset when one of them (the blue one) disappeared. We are not together, we are not whole, where the hell did that damn cat drop my little blue guy? I need the turtles to be together. The blue turtle was an adoptee, the other two a bit of a set. The blue one was solo and had belonged to no one. I scooped him up and he came with us. The turtles pre-date my current charges.

Cheddar needed out, he was going crazy. He was licking himself to death, he was eating paper, he was absconding with little blue turtles that never did him a lick of harm.

I look out the screen door. It is no use to wonder when this will all be over. I need to find a way to get back to my old life, MY life as best I can with my entourage as it is. This hellhole isn't selling, though. I look to the cat.

When we get to LA, I will get you a little buddy to play with. My buddies are there, too. We will have help with Grandpa. Grandpa will sit under a lemon tree. We just need to sell this shack as soon as possible and get all of us out. Stop licking your leg. I am calling the vet again tomorrow. I am calling the realtor tomorrow. Where the fuck did you drop my blue turtle?

Wasps

The wasps' nest hangs out of sight in the window. It is
smaller than last year's. I caught it in time. I have nightmares about
last year's. Big, buzzing, I didn't detect it until a few wasps decided
to stray from their cozy palace and Blue-Angel it into my room.
Cheddar and I howled and fled. I tip-toed back in, armed with a
rolled-up magazine and a spray bottle of some deadly (I am hoping)
Dollar Store cleanser. (I suspect the bargain brand cleanser couldn't
kill bacteria on the nasty sponge in the sink, much less a needle-y
squadron of wasps.) Where the hell are these things coming from?
There are no open windows in my room. I look around the room. I
look around again.

It has been forty years since I lived in this room. There was a partition back then, a flimsy wall-ish thing dividing the room for my brother and I. Partition being long gone, my mother moved into this room after the thrill of the romance was gone with my father. I don't know exactly when this occurred as I paid little attention to this house or anything that occurred here after I fled for my life to New York City after high school.

Other than the wall coming down, apparently no restorations or repairs have been made here in the years since I left. The floor is uneven, cobwebs hang, ancient computer equipment lurks, eyeing me balefully, just daring me to pick it up (better get those gloves on) and throw it out.

Hey, after you left, she moved in here, she wrote weird stuff and researched nut-job religions with us, and you are JUST NOW coming back and purging? Go ahead, pick us up, throw us out.

I eye the green, tattered plastic window shades. There are four windows, all with those green shades. All dusty, torn. None completely go up or down. Leading us back to the wasps. I didn't see the nest because the shade did not pull all the way up. I ripped it up and over the top sill and there it was.

I am irrationally afraid of the nest. I am afraid of the ugly horror of it. I am afraid of the black and gray of it. I am afraid of the little pockets, honeycombs which hold stinging, flying death. (This room is, has always been, stinging, flying death.) I aim the cleanser nozzle through a crack in the window and start blasting like I am in a Tarantino movie. Stinging, flying death, angry now, slithers from the pods and look for escape. There is none, I blast until I empty the chamber (well, until I am out of Filth Be Gone). Revved up now, singularly focused, I hop in the pick-up and head to the store. There I pick up the big guns, the Raid. No more playing around with second-rate weaponry. I speed back, running on pure adrenaline, and finish the job. Now I am left on the battlefield, bodies strewn about me, and though it is Mission Accomplished, I am still so afraid of the spooky, creepy nest I mewlingly call my nephew to come over and knock it down from the outside.

Dad, did you ever have wasps like this before? I show him the nest.

No, dear, not that I remember.

No, he doesn't remember.

That ratty shade still in place, I caught this year's nest before it grew too large. A couple of Raid squirts, and the few tenants were, er, evicted. The little nest is there, and scaring me still with its horror in miniature. Another call to the nephew.

I need to find a little peace in this room. If I clean, repair things, it means I live here, this is happening to me, this is happening to him. I acknowledge it. No, this is temporary, not happening. The house is on the market As Is. That means we are almost gone, right? We can leave soon, right? I can take him to live out the last years without stinging, flying death following us? We can leave the dead nest, and her, here.

Two Legs and a Twat

Scotty called it Two Legs and a Twat? It was always in the form of a question. In California, whenever I would bitch about a crappy day job, rickety actor cars and/or not getting the eighth supporting role in some shitty play in a rat-hole he would look at me and say, Mary, do you have two legs and twat?

Our standards for survival were extremely low in those days, but yes, back then, I had to grudgingly admit that I could possibly muster up a couple of walking things and maybe a relatively functioning girl thing. So, we could actually soldier on, we weren't as badly off as we liked to think we were, others had it worse, blah blah. Get on with it.

Dad sits and stares out the window for hours and hours at a time. He has relatively recovered from a recent fall, but since then I have noticed he has zero interest in doing anything but smoking. Dad, why don't we go for a ride, we can go down by the lake. Dad, let's go to dinner, we can go to that Italian place you like. Dad, let's go visit Aunt Carol, it's been awhile since you have seen her. Isn't there anywhere you want to go, Dad?

No, he says. I've seen it all. He actually says, 'I've seen it all.'

Hmm, really? You've seen it all? You're well enough to go out, but won't (two legs and a twat?).

This shutdown distresses me immensely but my advisors up here assure me it is completely normal and part of the Alzheimer's progression. He is pretty far advanced now, they tell me. They tell me a lot of things, helpful things, were I in the frame of mind to hear any of it. In my panic and fury at this horrific disease, I rage.

Would it kill you to get up from the goddamn chair and go to the fucking lake with me? Go out and look at the fucking robins hopping on the fucking lawn? You've got two legs and a twat, don't you, Mary? Would it kill you to try to live?

Of course, all unsaid, all just lightning bolts shooting around inside my head. I nod my head, murmur something along the lines of, Ok, Daddy, maybe tomorrow.

Because the fact of the matter is, he doesn't have two legs and a twat anymore. Neither does Scotty, on my shoulder much these days, but dead a year now.

Yeah, I suppose I am stuck here, away from my tribe, helplessly watching this play out and assisting as I can. With surgeries, an old, mean cat, a hell shack in constant need of something, crying over a lost job, a lost identity, crying over Bobby, Teddy, Sally, the neighbor dog and the cow next door all probably not loving me as much anymore, I do, in fact possess two legs and a twat, Mary.

I drive to the lake.

Child Star Dies

Child Star Dies. Of course I click on the headline. (I am so old now, the only celebs I recognize anymore are child stars.) Some mister from *Old Yeller*. I didn't recognize the name. The oldest kid, was that the main kid who belonged to *Old Yeller?* Or was that the youngest kid? How many kids were there, anyway?

Old Fucking Yeller. I look down at the keyboard.

I was older than 6, maybe 8. So that would have put Larry at 6. It was a cold, windy, snowy night in Ashland, Maine (that's how I remember all the nights in Ashland, though) and *Old Yeller* had finally come to the movie theatre in Presque Isle. The Big Town. Down the winding mountain road from our little hamlet to where everything glittered. We were going to the movies and that was a very glamourous occasion in Northern Maine. Except last minute my brother, Larry was not allowed to go. He had been bed-wetting, and as punishment, my mother wouldn't let him go. I can still hear him crying. He cried and cried. I could see my mother felt badly at this and suspected she rued this particular hard whammy. She had not descended into her own hell yet (well, not totally).

She still managed to function somewhat and still could muster up a touch of that 'ole Oh-yeah-I-got-two-little-kids-and-I-probably-need-to-care-about-that feeling every now and then. She often forgot she had two little kids, (hmm, think that's gonna be a problem down the line?) but I could see now that she was sorrowful about Larry's distress.

Fuck him, I was not. I was delighted that he was being punished. Only Dad and I were going on this thrilling expedition. Nothing was more satisfying to an eight-year old girl than for her enemies to be vanquished. As the car pulled away, I could still hear him wailing and I somehow remember the rather forlorn look on my mother's usually fearsome face.

I don't remember much more about that night. We probably got snacks; I probably cried when Old Yeller was (spoiler-alert) shot. I don't remember which kid the now-dead Child Star was. I don't remember even if there was more than one kid. I do remember being out alone with Daddy, the favorite parent, the absent (idealized) parent. I remember the sweet victory.

I thought of Old Yeller off and on throughout the years. On the rare occasions back to town, (town being where everyone but me now lived in Massachusetts, long away from Maine) I sometimes would think Larry and I should rent *Old Yeller*. I would wonder if he ever got to see it. Did he see it with his own kids?

Dad's diagnosis came a little before Larry's. Larry and I would talk about how to handle him doddering around, and now doddering around with dementia. Jesus, would one of us have to move back in with him? Which one of us?

Better you than me, bub. You're closer, you're better suited, I'm a city person, well, we have to do something, OK we can figure it out together, it's not too bad yet, he's still driving, he will be OK on his own for awhile longer, we have to get him to stop smoking, though, that is a little scary, yeah, I guess it's OK for now, can't the kids check on him more often? It's not too bad yet.

I was sitting around the kitchen table, back in town to check on Dad, when Larry's news came in. The prognosis had been pending for several months, none of us really wanting to know. I put the phone down and tell Dad. I can see it doesn't really register fully, which I am somewhat thankful for.

I feed the cat, fold the laundry and call Dad to the bathroom. The disease has progressed as expected, though the ride is no less unsettling. Same routine twice a day and he doesn't remember from one panty change to the next what the drill is. Odd, how it is really only the bathroom stuff where he completely blanks and needs the most supervision.

C,mon Dad, we are doing your toilette and then we are going out to dinner, so we need to move things along. It will be fun to go out, huh?

Oh yes, dear.

So, OK, (after panty change), you need to wash your hands with hot water and soap and then we will go.

I leave the door ajar and sit at the kitchen table, always within earshot. It's he and I and the cat now, and neither of those two will be helpful brainstorming as to how to winterize this shack.

Do I get reams of saran wrap and strap it over windows and take a blow dryer to it? Is there more to it than that? Jesus.

What the hell is taking so long in there? I poke my head in. He has started to shave, a lengthy process for him. Fuck.

Dad, we need to be out in a few minutes because we need to be at the restaurant. Goddamn it. Fuck. I knew I should have stayed right on him. What the fuck is he thinking about shaving now for?

Dad, you are going to have to speed that up because we really need to go. *If you aren't out of that bathroom in five minutes, you are not going to Old Yeller, mister, do I make myself clear?*

He looks at me, a little mystified. I help him shave.

I bundle him up and we drive off into another cold, windy night; Dad and I again off to where something glittered.

Supermarket Roses

I was harried and had a million things to do. Driving back
from my father's rehab facility I went another way, a different way
than GPS had told me. I was tired of GPS. I had a load of his
laundry in the back, I had to do that before I left town. I had to shop,
contact the different doctors, get the cat ready. I had to find clothes
to take back to him. Do I need to tell the VA people he is now in
this place rather than that place? Fuck, I probably do. One more
thing and time was running out. I am hungry, when was the last time
I ate anything? Speed up. This road looks familiar, was I just here
with Marie? This road comes into that big intersection by Larry's
old place. Does it, can that be right? No, just hurry up. But it does
look familiar. It looked familiar when I was with here with Marie

last week. I wanted to say something to her about it at the time. I should have talked to her then. Fuck yep, that's the intersection. Just roll by it. I roll by it fast, I don't even look. I have been meaning to go by the house for two years. There never has been time, I don't want to see it, should I bring Dad by it? He doesn't even remember anymore, why push my luck with that. Well I am sure as hell not going by today. I am safely by, I slow down. Around the bend. Fuck. The Big Y. I forgot that was right around the corner. I have never been able to go by that without drama either. I don't have time for that, either. I pull in, I sit in the parking lot. No. Not time now. Get home, take care of the mechanics. You don't need to see the house or think about that night in the store right now. Not while your last remaining family member is in the hospital.

I pull out of the parking lot and turn the car around. Fuck, who has time for this shit? I'm starving. I wonder if I can stop at the pho place when I FINALLY get back on the road to the house.

Do I even remember Larry's address? Simone Drive, that was it. Or was it Simone Road? Do I need to pull out the phone and fuck with the GPS? No, part of this exercise has always been 'can

you find the house by your nose?' Dad always knew the way, he
and I would go over there sometimes, even when she was alive,
without her. I don't think she ever went. We had a great time, Dad
and I riding over there, we would laugh and gossip. She was pretty
far gone by then, lost in her mind and hatred. We loved leaving her
to go to Larry's. I loved even more leaving them all to go back to
NY/LA, wherever I was at the time. Didn't matter, it was good to
not be there. Now that I mention it, Larry was pretty far gone
himself when he had that house, turning into her. Alcoholism,
despair, I noticed he treated his own kids the way she was with Larry
and me. No matter, the drive was fun, Dad and I.

Was it right here? Before the big intersection I can see up
ahead? Fuck, I turned too soon. Do I need the gps? No, without it,
you can do it without it. Just make a left up here, I am sure to
recognize something up ahead. YES, that little mini mart on the left.
YES! That is right, I remember that. Keep straight. I wonder if that
diner is up here, what was it, AL's, Frank's? Larry's then wife and I
took the kids here once. Why did we take the kids and not Larry?
Before the divorce, the kids were small, and we are somehow at this
diner. Maybe Larry was fucked, maybe that was why we had the

kids out. Before the divorce. There it is, up ahead on the right. Looks exactly the same. Al's. Old timey 50's. I pass and now remember exactly how to get to the house. Up this hill, steep curvy. That sharp right, around the bend. Christ I am hungry. What is the point of this? Why do I want to see the house? I don't know.

Nine years earlier, from New York City, on a Tuesday night, I barked into the phone, Is she dead yet?

No not yet, Dad and I just left the hospital, Larry says.

I had flown all day from LA and was now back at my old apartment on 89th. The Massachusetts leg of the journey would have to wait until the morning. By morning, though, she WAS dead. (None of that bullshit 'wait for your loved one to arrive from a far-flung place to say goodbye and die nicely' for her, no sirree. Fine by me.) I loaded onto Amtrak headed north. Larry met me at the station and we headed to dad's house.

We went over the death details. The hospital wanted to know if we wanted to go over and view the body before it was sent to the funeral home. Thanks, anyway, but we're good on that. Larry and I were to meet with the funeral director at 2:00, bring over clothes, crunch the funeral numbers, etc... Dad had passed on this, it was falling to Larry and I. Dad had earlier pulled me aside in the kitchen.

I've hated her for forty years, I'm glad she's dead.

I hear you, bub, but we may want to tamp that down for the grandkids sake, and I think Larry is taking it harder than expected. So, you and I should probably zip it until we get through the service on Friday.

Thursday, Dad and I take the drive over to the Simone Road Drive house (left at that gas station, you want coffee at the diner?) to work on the funeral, reception details. I knew we were in trouble the minute we opened the door. Larry must have been drinking since the moment he opened his eyes. I looked at dad and he sighed. We worked on details during the day, but as day turned into endless night, a drunk boy spun and spun and spun.

I have the day off from work tomorrow, all my office people are coming to the service, I want everyone at the service to have a rose, I want roses to be presented to dad by the grave, I have the day off from work tomorrow, all my office people are coming to the service, I want everyone at the service to have a rose, I want

roses to be presented to dad by the grave.

Shut up, Larry, you're drunk, we get it. And we are not

doing that rose presentation bullshit. Maybe the throngs of mourners

can each have a rose or something if that's what it takes to shut you

up.

Now, it's late and we still have a shopping trip to the nearby

supermarket, the Big Y down by that funky intersection. All

supplies have to be loaded in for the reception at the Simone Road

Drive house. Larry wanted everybody back to the house for a

barbeque and now we have to shop for all this crap. (A side note;

why the fuck am I worrying about ribs and coleslaw, aren't people

supposed to be bringing over covered dishes and shit? Is this

America? I should be up to my tits in mac and cheese and tuna

casseroles brought by caring neighbors.)

Ok, we must go now and get all this shit and you aren't

driving, you are too drunk. At this point, a fight ensues over how

exactly how drunk he is.

I am not drunk, I can too drive, I am going, you can't stop

me the usual tired belligerent blah blah of all tired belligerent drunks everywhere in the world. The argument is escalating between he and I, and as I glance over at my niece, his daughter, and catch her sad, frightened eyes, my father rises. He walks to Larry and puts his arms out. Saying not a word, he gathers up his son. It's been a hard week, you did the best you could, why don't you go lie down now?

Larry starts sobbing uncontrollably. I AM too drunk, you're right, he says to me. You guys go, don't forget the roses. Dad hugs him for a while longer and steers him to the stairs.

The three of us hike back to the supermarket.

Dad, this rose fuckery he wants is really making me want to puke. We should just get them, though, huh?

Yes.

We get stuff and stuff and stuff, pre-made tubs of potato salad and more stuff. (Goddamnit could it have killed ONE of the neighbors to send over funeral food, a Jell-o salad that one gags down at these things, ANYTHING?) And roses. A few sad little bunches of cellophaned and wilty-looking roses.

You mark this night, my lady, I remember thinking to myself. Jesus Christ, a woman's life comes down to tubs of potato salad, a non-existent neighborly green bean casserole, and supermarket roses. You will be paying for this night for a long time to come, remember it. On some level I knew then it would sear my psyche.

After the service the next day (roses were handed out and tossed on the coffin, but Dad and I won the no-presentation battle), Dad and I drove away, back the old familiar way. It was the last time I was in the house.

Larry has been gone almost two years himself now. Every time I pass that intersection taking Dad to a doctor's appointment, I feel a physical spasm every time I pass the Big Y. I have wanted to remember where Larry lived. I have wanted to make sense of the rose run that night, that night my father was kind to his little drunk boy.

I make the right turn around the bend, yep this is right. There is Helene's on the corner. Larry and I used to stop there and load up on cigarettes and coffee cake before we went to the house. I cruise around the cul de sac and there it is. 34 Simone Drive Road. It has been painted, it looks sprightly. I stop in front. The blinds are drawn. I don't need to stay long. As I pull away I catch a glimpse of a swing set in the back yard.

When I bring Dad back to the house, I will drive this way, past the Big Y. Maybe I won't seize up then. Dad won't remember the funeral rose, potato salad run. He won't recognize the turn off road to Larry's house. I am extraordinarily lucky that he doesn't ask for Larry anymore. He used to, and I would have to tell him all over again that Larry had passed. Now he has forgotten, hopefully for good.

Do I Need to Shave My Legs for This?

Prelude – 9 AM Dylan Day

She picks me up at 9:00AM. I slide into the car, nervously adjusting a shawl, or something. Nervously adjusting something. She tells me later she thought the day could go either way. Yes, either way though, at the time I was leaning 60/40 my way.

What is happening? What time are you seeing him?

Around 2:00. Whenever I get Dad settled after lunch. I have arranged for Bella to come in tonight to take care of him.

The last few visits with the man in the north had lasted until well into the night. He was helping me with something. I needed his help. Lila contacted him for me when I asked. He agreed to see

44

me. He agreed to help. I was wary of any contact, initially. I wanted him to help me via email, via google docs, via anything at all except meeting. Except talking IRL, as the kids say. Neither of us were kids. It had been many years since we had crossed paths. I thought of him from time to time.

I had heard he was fragile. He's fucked up, be careful. Yes, I'll be careful. (I'm fucked up, too, how fucked up could he be?)

Pretty fucked up, actually.

Lila and I go to the café. I am never up this early to go anywhere; it's a miracle I am here. I nervously adjust something again.

What do you think, she asked me? I think maybe, I tell her.

Wow, she says. Who would have thought?

I know. Certainly not me.

Well, she says. Text me as soon as you can, let me know.

Do you think I should shave my legs for this? I ask?

Betty, I'd shave everything, she says.

Yes. Shave everything.

He and I had a few sessions where he helped me with the thing. There was an immediate connection. We worked on the thing

45

until late in the night on most occasions. He was recently single after a break-up of a long term relationship. I was not so recently single. I was single for a long time now. I was a late middle-aged woman living with her father with Alzheimer's and a cat in a barely habitable shit shack on the outskirts of a small town. I was a cross between Norman Bates and Annie Wilkes.

He kissed me goodbye in the parking lot that first time we met. He was attentive, he was complimentary of the thing I asked him for help with. He made coffee, I brought sweets. He gave me little presents, he mailed me things he had picked up for me (to help with the thing).

He also talked a lot about how fucked up he was. He spoke largely of what he was doing to counter the fucked-up-ness. I listened.

That's what I do best, listen. In retrospect, I should have known better. It was never about me, and I, needy and starved for any kind of attention, knew that deep down. I felt a twinge of shame as I girlishly fussed over outfits and make-up to prep for visits. Stupid, really. No way is he capable of anything other than getting out of bed, though tremendous help he was with the thing. I knew this and yet changed outfits three times, bought new lipstick, stopped

a mile from his house to gather myself before I drove in. And, oh,

yeah, I worked doubly hard on the thing. Regardless of the personal

bullshit, the thing was really taking off and he was a huge part of

this.

I have always lived pretty firmly in the world of self-

delusion. Never really believing fully in my circumstances, ever,

has served me relatively well. Now, in particular, with the addled

father, cat, shitshack, self delusion swirled around me like a well

worn caftan. None of this is happening, and in my head I often had

conversations with others, known and unknown, that made the

circumstances bearable.

Lila asks me, What time are you getting there?

Yeah, I gotta get going, I have a million things to do before I

head up. I pick up sweet things before we leave the café.

I had better run home and shave my legs, I (half) jokingly say

to Lila.

Oh, yes, Betty, you had better, you never know. Text me

when you can.

I think about my already shaved legs on the ride back to the house.

Two Days before Dylan Day

Unbeknownst to Lila, I had researched waxing palaces a few days ago. I had asked my hairdresser betty at the salon, in a bit of a whisper, where (in this godforsaken fucking blip of an afterthought of a town) can I get a bikini wax? I am used to big town salons on every corner where I can get nails done and every body part I want waxed at any time, not this shithole little town where I'm thinking maybe the pussy-waxing market isn't as large. I asked nicer than that. I asked her, So where around these parts can I get my nails done and a bikini wax? Hmm, she thought. Let me see. No, nowhere in town, but let me ask Jane. Jane will know. I look around the salon. I watch Elise glide through my hair clippings and over to world weary, all knowing Jane. Elise bends over, whispers in her ear. Jane looks up and over at me. She looks over at Elise and says something slowly, carefully. Elise scuttles back over. Next town over, Regina's Nails, I think they also wax.

48

Great, thanks! Gee, I'm surprised there isn't a place closer, though.

Well, she says, you know, the next town over... College Town.

Ah, yes, College Town. That's where I need to be.

Next day I head over to College Town. I'm seeing him in two days. I need to get this done.

How fucking stupid is this whole thing, really? Did I need to really feel this stupid about it? Just do it. It won't kill you anyway, just do it. Hey, you never know.

I pull into the shopping mall in College Town where Regina's Nails beckons, blinks. I see Asian women in the windows. Good, it looks like it is the same thing as a city joint where you walk in, grab a color, then later somebody leads you to the back where they throw a sheet over you and 1-2-3. That's what I remember, anyway. I poke my head in-somebody looks up while brandishing an emery board. I need my nails done and a bikini wax.

No, no, she says, we don't do that here. Maybe down the road.

Fuck. This is stupid. I am so wrong about this-this is confusing and weird. How badly am I misreading this situation? He is so fucked up. I am so fucked up. These long nights are strange. He has that recovering alcoholic penchant for focusing, fixating on other areas of life. I never, never should have let this get this far, I knew better. I should have trusted myself more on this. I should have listened, all I wanted was to email over pages, have him edit and email the edits back. I never, ever wanted to get this personally involved with him, I did not want him to be this personally involved with my work. I knew this would happen, It's on me. It's not on him. My fault. I am pathetically lonely and when he kissed me in the parking lot...

There have been signs I have been unable to read. Did I mistake the kiss, did I misread those long, excruciating nights as interest? Well, wait, you mainly listened to his drama. You listened and listened. I clucked and murmured and did I even wipe away a fuckin tear of his? Jesus Cathy, off the bat this has been more about him. How many times are you going to be this stupid and vulnerable to men? How many more men will treat you offhandedly-as a prop to be grabbed off the backstage table as he (they) make another entrance?

Well, he's helping. So what? I DO need the help, my participles are dangling; its, it's, whom or who? I need help cleaning that-a very dispassionate job of an editor, and now you are driving around looking for pussy waxing places. What the fuck happened between A and B on that spectrum? You're wrong, you're really wrong. Even though he says I am saving him, even though he says I do him more good than he does me–you're wrong. He doesn't really mean it. Men don't really mean it.

I head on up the road, a little ways out of College Town. I pull into the lot of the salon where Regina has referred me. Yes, a high-end looking little swanky place. Discreet signage, all things possible here at Gossamer. I sit in the truck. I am sitting in a pick-up, behind a cornfield, in front of a salon called Gossamer ready to step inside to inquire about a bikini wax because I am anticipating a possible liaison with my old, retired, recovering alcoholic, train wreck high school English teacher who (whom?) is immensely talented and a huge help in editing the book and worth whom (who?) I probably had a slight crush on in school and now, forty years later, am thrown together in a confusing tornado of pent up longings and sorrows and needs and regrets. Do I have that right? Is that the current situation?

I sit in the truck. I don't go in. I think about, and am ashamed of, my previous mental condemnation of unwaxed farmer's wives, everywhere. Simply untrue, my assessments of who waxes and who doesn't. I am angry and furiously lashing out at the imaginary rubes I have in my head, I don't know any farmer's wives. I know nice, kind people who help me every chance they get. My fury at my current predicament knows no bounds, and, while I could feel the rage start to choke me back at Regina's, I sit motionless in the truck and whimper.

In reality, the last time was a few years back, in Lexington Avenue, in preparation for another train wreck. I ducked into a storefront, a stern looking matriarch shooshed me to the back, threw me a johnnie, and dispatched with bikini hair in under 15 minutes. And then I waited over the four day Memorial Day weekend for a call that never came. This is going to be equally fucked up with him, and now my work is involved, too. Fuck.

I get out of the truck. I go in, walk down the stairs. I step up to the receptionist. I ask, she tells. Tomorrow, Caitlin, 4:00. $40.

Ok, fine. I walk back to the truck. Good. I am seeing him the day after, so check that off the to-do list. What is still on the to-do list is reviewing the pages I am taking over to him for edit. So, a little less time worrying about pruning your pussy and a lot more time worrying about pruning your documents.

One Day Before Dylan Day

Next day I pull in to Gossamer around 3:45. I go down the steps, sign in and wait politely. A perky betty bounds out, greets me and leads me back to a spa room. She, assuming I know, remember, the procedure, hands me a robe and leaves. I undress and sit on the table. The room is fancier than the storefront on Lexington. Unidentifiable potion jars line the wall and crock pot looking thing of wax looks like it should be bubbling. The carpet is a plush beige, plants hang in the corners. Enya-ish new age music is pumped in. Brochures, pamphlets are strewn artfully over a table. You too, and your new pretty pussy can be frolicking on this beach!

Caitlin strides in. A young, stout, tattooed Irish woman, she gets right down to it. Throw one leg over here, one over there. Ouch, God almighty that is hot. Ouch, Jesus Christ that hurts. I know she says, once you start coming in regularly, it will hurt less. Shall we do Brazilian? We might as well, Caitlin, I'm here, right? OK, turn over, throw one leg here, and then again. Flip over, now the other leg here, now there.

Who DOES this type of work? I ask her about herself. She is in school, with a big family. Six sisters. I ask who her typical customer is? Farmer's wives? College girls, she says. Ahh, College Town, of course. She asked me, Why are you doing this? New boyfriend, I lie. I hear myself say it. New boyfriend. Jesus. Oh she says, I told my boyfriend, I'm waxing, but not for you, bud. I do it for myself. I look at her. I throw another leg somewhere else. Oh yes, she says, do it for yourself.

Yes, do it for myself. Yes, for myself.

I thank her. I throw her an exorbitant tip.

I clamber, gingerly, back into the pick-up. Caitlin had warned me that things were going to be raw, painful and unpretty for a day or so. Of course, dummy, a day before any encounter is not nearly enough time to heal. So, tomorrow might not be the day anyway. Start thinking that tomorrow might not be the day for a lot of reasons.

Do it for yourself.

It's done. I did it. I drive home, foolishly.

6 AM Dylan Day

I call them Dylan days. I wake up and Oh, it's a Dylan Day. I usually have arranged for the aide to come in in the evening, but there is always always this goddamned bullshit that has to be done. All the errands that have to be run. Food, meds, panty changes, all have to be coordinated for a fucking afternoon, evening out, never mind a few days, or even a week. Even a week, forget that. Forget a week. I try to do as much as I can before Dylan Day. Shop before, cook the day before. That way the aide just comes in, changes him, gives meds and she can just heat up whatever I have cooked. Easy. But it takes a lot of prep. A lot of prep to escape for the afternoon, maybe the evening. Who knows? Maybe the whole night? The whole night? Yes, I can get back in the morning before he gets up. I can get home before he really gets going for the day, I can get home, be ready to change him, give pills, slop out the piss bucket, mop the floor. I can do all that in the morning. Yes, all that in the morning.

A Dylan Day (or any other Escape Day) is a lot of work. The ratio is usually 2:1. Two Prep Days for one Dylan Day.

No matter now, though, as Dylan Day dawns. I lie there, listening, waiting. I like to lie and think about the Day to come. As long as I am in bed, the day doesn't come. I can anticipate the day. The day can unfold any way I want it to unfold, in my head. It is a busy day, in my head. I wait, I don't hear anything. Lila has said she will pick me up for breakfast before I head north. I haven't told her about the Wax Palace search the past two days. I reach down, smooth, raw, stupid. I don't think I will tell her. That might indicate a hopefulness that I don't think she shares. I may have over anticipated this and I am far too embarrassed to confess this to her. She is kind to take me to breakfast this morning as I know she knows this particular Dylan Day is a Turning Point Day. This will go one way or the other. Live or Die today.

Live, and be married with a nice writerly life up north and happily adjusted to taking care of dear old dad in a nursing home or wherever we decide to put him, together. Go with Dylan to meetings (God, he still goes daily after thirteen years), bounce his grandkids on your knee. Ughh, I will be step-granny. Don't think about that, you can be the cool step-granny, look at it that way. You can be the granny the kids come to ask was it cool to be in New York City in the 70's? Do you know Iggy Pop?*

Or Die, spinster washed up Whatever Happened to Baby Jane used to be actor that looked after her father for thirty years until he died at 140 and her 80 year old cat ate her face off. Those were the only two ways this day was going to go. I'm not a shades of gray type person.

1 PM Dylan Day

I'm on the road and he texts me. Bring hot sauce, I'm making chili. Jesus Christ, I text Lila, he had dinner figured out. You think? she asked. This was a breakthrough. We had never eaten together. We had drunk a thousand cups of coffee; he has a sweet tooth, there were a million cookies. But never food. He is making chili, I text Lila, though, he hadn't mentioned dinner.

Maybe he was making chili for the church picnic, I don't know he is making dinner for me, he never said so. He is, Betty, Lila said. He is.

I pick up the hot sauce. I head north and stop in the usual place I stop at, ½ mile from his house. I always stop there, in a little turn around. I gulp water, I scarf down altoids, I fix my hair, re-apply lipstick, but not too much so it doesn't look like I put on lipstick to go see him for an editing session.

He is crunched over the crockpot when I arrive. We hug hello, he turns his head. He thanks me for the hot sauce; sprinkles some in the pot. We make coffee, spread out the cookies. We sit in the kitchen and talk about his meeting schedule. He announces he won't go tonight, he can stay and work with me. I discourage this, no problem I can be out by. No, no, that is OK, I am OK and the work we do together is helpful to him, gives him purpose. Ok, I say. If you're sure. We edit. Line by line. He tells me how good I am; he keeps saying he is not good enough to edit my work, he is a burnt out English teacher. Well, that's what I need, I say. You're not burnt out, I need an English teacher. I chose you for a reason. Is it who or whom? When do you spell out numbers; when can you just write the number? No, no, he says, this is easy, you don't need to worry about that, an editor will fix that for you. Somebody will see this stuff; somebody will read this, you'll be published. I'm not good enough. This goes on for quite a while.

Him, I'm not good enough for you.

Me, I chose you.

I can feel it slip away. I see there is nothing I can do. I reach down at one point and run my hand down my smooth, lotioned leg. I stop trying. I watch him twist. Ten hours later, we have gone over every line, fixed very wayward verb tense. Dinner is not mentioned. At 2AM, all hope gone, but with a blistering manuscript in my hand, I rise to leave. He, startled, dashed to the crockpot. Oh, it's burned, he says, I am sorry. I should have added water. (We burned chili in a crockpot, I didn't think that was even possible.) Oh, it's burned, he says again. Oh, too bad, I say, as I am still technically uninvited to dinner. Too bad for those church picnic-goers tomorrow, I guess.

He walks me out, I get straight into the pick-up and get home around 4AM.

There were a couple more phone calls, a few emails, though much less frequently.

I see him one more time. It was like that last burst of energy they say fading patients can have. Like, sitting upright in the hospital bed, ripping off the mask, eating a bowl of ice cream and then singing One Singular Sensation before sinking back and dying. Another epic editing session and this time he suggests we break for dinner. We go to the College Town, and I can see he is pleased to be with me; pleased to be seen with me. He slides in the banquette around to be sitting next to me. We talk about food. Do you like this? You don't like that? He chats with the couple at the next table, we laugh with the waiter. Normal people; we look like normal people. As we leave to go back to editing, he tells the couple next table over, She's a writer, we're working.

Yes. Back at it I say. Back at it we go.

A couple of texts more, a couple of emails, one more phone call, and that's it. We never speak or see each other again.

In the 70's, maybe early 80s, in New York City,

I had, in fact spoken to Iggy Pop a couple of times.

Sparkle Pads

I first noticed it on Halloween. I started to cramp, and not just any cramping. Cramping like when I was 14. I had terrible periods as a girl. Very painful, pukey, bleedy, all exacerbated by the very stressful living conditions as an adolescent girl coping with way more than she should be coping with. The misery tapered off a bit after I left home, figured out tampons, grew up, married and all that follows miserable adolescence, but not by much. And poof, just like that, at 38, I was done. I saw my gynecologist in New York City after some extreme cramping and bleeding and I was informed I was perimenopausal.

Huh, I said? I am 38, kinda young there, don't we think?

Well, it happens, they tell me.

Oh, thanks, yes, that is helpful, thanks for that. Uh huh.

So, in upstate New York, around Niagara Falls, as we were pulling out to drive across and move to Los Angeles, on the Fourth of July, I bled for the last time. Patriotic of me, I thought. For God and Country.

It didn't bother me in the least as I never planned on having children.

Oh God, no, I said to them all, husband and overnight Gentleman Callers. Nuh Uh, misters, you do INDEED need to get up and find an open Duane Reed's before you're graced (while I use drugstore run-time to dust off the diaphragm and move that northward). Double Protect-No Worries tattooed in a thigh somewhere.

I never bled in California, except during the dark nights of the soul, and (usually) those dark nights of the soul don't send you wandering down the Savon aisles looking for feminine products. But here, twenty years later, in Massachusetts, on Halloween, I was bleeding. And not just bleeding, hemorrhaging as if I were miscarrying Rosemary's Baby. On Halloween. Unnerved, the next day I pulled my friend Lila aside.

What the fuck, Lila, with this? Is this weird?

Lila, healthcare professional that she is, says, Uh, Betty, you need to call Dr. Someone, and you need to call Dr. Someone today.

Jesus, huh? Yes, I do. I will. I call Dr. Someone.

They get me in in a few days.

Meanwhile, still bleeding here, Lila tells me what painkiller to buy for the cramping and I head for the local equivalent of Duane Reed/Savon to buy, well, what? I get to the 'feminine health' aisle. I wander up and down, open-mouthed. Things have changed in the twenty years since that fateful Buffalo Fourth of July (God and Country) last period. What are the 14-year-old girls wearing now? Back then there was only the mattress pad-like thing you strapped on using that weird belt that rather resembled a parachute. Tampons were out as I was not sure that was the safest way to go as my entire womb seemed to be looking for the exit doors. So, here I was, elbowing aside tweens, as we all perused sanitary napkin options. Only, they aren't called sanitary napkins anymore, like your mother and her farty friends called them. I walk up and down the aisle just staring at the array. There had to be twenty different kinds of pads for 14-year-old (58-year-olds) Maxi, mini, slender, winged,

Unicorns, non-winged, pink, scented, Princess Purple, My Little Pony Pads, unscented, glittered, sparkle pads. I lunge forward and grab the orange sparkle pads. I stagger back to the house, down a handful of Tylenol and wrestle with the wings.

Oh my God what if I have cervical cancer? Just my luck who will take care of him, what will I do with him, there isn't anyone to send him to. Not to be too whiny about it, but can I catch a fucking break here? OK, what if it is cervical cancer, but not REALLY BAD cervical cancer? What if I just have to go into the hospital awhile, and then come out and take some drugs? That wouldn't be so bad, right? I have 30 days respite care for him, if I go into the hospital for under 30 days, I can get him out and we will both take it from there. If this drama is bad I need to figure out what happens with him. Of course I won't tell him anything now. Who DO I tell, actually? Lila knows. Nobody else, I can tell nobody else. Really no reason to say anything to anybody until at least after I see Dr. Someone and we have a clearer picture as to what the fuck.

I see the doctor and it is decided I need to undergo a surgical biopsy, outpatient, at a local hospital. That is a little more complicated than I wanted to deal with, but, yes, given some previous circumstances, the surgical option was the best way to go.

At this point I tell people, only four or so. Friends who murmur,

there, there. Often a good, solid there, there can do the trick. I hold

off telling my father I am going in for a surgical procedure until the

last minute as I know he won't be able to understand precisely what

is happening. He will understand the hospital part of the explanation

and that would make him uneasy. I arrange for a trusted aide to

come in and care for him the evening of the procedure as I know I

won't be up for it.

The hospital folks make you have someone drive you to and

from. I try to argue my way out of that.

Oh, I'll be fine, I can make it back to the house. Will I bleed

a lot on the way back? If so, I will double up on the Sparkle Pads

and throw a horse blanket on the seat, no problem.

They didn't go for that, mumbling about anesthesia,

recovery rooms and drugs. They also got insistent on emergency

contacts, which I currently did not have.

Jesus fucking Christ I don't have an emergency contact.

What if something god-awful happens during the procedure? What

if I bleed out on the table? Unlikely, yes, but the medical folks have been bugging me about an emergency contact for the last year. Nobody here who needs to know if something god-awful happens, I always thought. Anyhow, I am never going to be here long enough to need an emergency contact. HA! I am only here until I can figure out this Alzheimer's thing with my father and when I figure that out I won't be here anymore so no need for emergency contact here in New England. Soon, I will be back to my life and people in the west, where there are PLENTY of emergency contacts don't you worry about that one little bit Jesus fucking Christ what if I have fucking cervical cancer?

Lila, without being asked, announced she was taking the day off and would take custody of me that day. Driving, waiting, talking to doctors, she made food for that evening for my dad and I. Lila, my emergency contact; the show runner. I give her the names of people she should contact, east and west, should anything really god-awful happen. (Not really at the appointment, not to be all drama queen-y about it, the procedure should be fine, but more in case of me skidding into an icy ditch in these hellish winters.)

Jesus fucking Christ what if I have fucking cervical cancer? That's one of the worst ones, isn't it? Jesus I always knew that old

66

man would be the last man standing. How funny, the irony of it. He buries me, no, I am not being buried, cremation. I have to start writing this shit down somewhere, don't I? Lila has the people to call, fuck, I forgot to give her my cousins' information. I should do that, the cousins are really the only blood family left, at least, the only blood family I would want to know if anything bad happens, what if I bleed out on the table, what if my father outlives me, did I just bleed through a fucking sparkle pad what if I have fucking cervical cancer?

Lila pulls up that morning, all smiles and radiating confidence. I pile into the seat beside her, relieved. The last surgery, two years ago, a much bigger, complicated affair, found me alone day of the surgery, puking into a recovery room bucket, wheeled into a Roosevelt Hospital room and parked with an elderly, deranged roommate who howled 'help me help me at the top of her lungs all night. Finally, and may the gods forgive me, I very loudly started shouting Just go towards the light, Grandma. Jesus just walk faster towards the light. I kicked up such a fuss I made them move me to another room. Point being, no fun having to advocate for yourself in the hospital when one is not really in the best shape to do so.

I have fasted the night before, no food, water, nothing until after the surgery. I offer Lila twenty bucks to stop for coffee. I don't need food, but I do need coffee. We talk about how it is worse somehow when you are forbidden to eat or drink. I normally don't eat before noon anyway, but being told I can't makes me want to gnaw my leg off. Coffee, though, that we need now.

$25?

No.

We arrive. We park. We roll through the admission process. They lead us back into the surgical waiting area, a nurse's station with cubicles, bays, for patients pre-and post-surgical.

Now things happen faster. I am ushered to a bed near the nurse's station. Thankfully Lila is allowed to stay with me so far; she settles in a chair next to me; a crossword is pulled out.

June, a gruff-ish nurse barks at me.

Take that off. Put this on.

I immediately take it off and put that on. Scrambling a bit, June reaches for the curtain to pull around the bed, chair and monitors that have been rolled into our bay.

Don't worry, honey, please, I'm show folk and have been naked in more backstage dressing rooms across the country than I can remember.

Gruff June laughs. Lila, not looking up from her crossword, snorts. Lila and Gruff June start to talk around me as I fall back on the bed and wrestle with the hairnet thing I have been presented with. My hair is all of a sudden very long and I can't get it all into the hairnet thing. It keeps falling out, my hands are shaking.

Jesus fucking Christ what if I have cervical fucking cancer?

Gruff June and Lila are talking about their local church parishes. I hear June say she could never go to confession with a younger priest.

Now, old Father Mike, he was alright, one time I...

Jesus fucking Christ what if I...?

I want coffee. I offer Gruff June a hundred bucks.

No.

Jayne, another nurse comes in, wheeling more equipment. More questions, and for some reason, one has to announce one's birthday to each new medic. Jayne starts to affix wired-up tabs all over me to get something something vital signs.

I start to separate.

Lila asks, Who wrote Robinson Crusoe?

Fuck, who DID write Robinson Crusoe? Jayne and I look at each other. C'mon, we are smart women, who the hell wrote Robinson Crusoe? I look at Lila. Is it possible, that between the three of us, we don't know that.

Dafoe Lila says. She says she turned over the puzzle to the answers on the back.

Willem Dafoe wrote Robinson Caruso? Huh? No, that's probably not right.

My doctor comes in, introduces himself to my posse. We speak briefly about how this all will roll, he tells me the anesthesiologist will be in shortly to talk to me about sedation. He talks about sedation as opposed to full on general anesthesia. The conversation goes quickly, I hear about half of it. Lila asks questions. He says he will see me soon and goes to suit up. Gruff

70

June remarks that my doctor is fourteen and then wanders over to the nurse's station. Jayne starts unhooking me and I smell imminent surgery in the air. I offer her $200 for coffee.

Hey Gruff June, the offer over here is now $200 for coffee. Do you want in on this, or are you going to leave Jayne here to snap that up?

What the fuck was the difference again between full on general anesthesia and just being sedated? I can't recall. Lila tells me. Oh, OK. I can see she is leaning toward sedation. Easier to bounce back, wake up from. With general, yeah, I remember now, I tend to puke. It took me longer to wake up and I puked a lot. Yes, sedation. Even though I am afraid of being in the least bit conscious if it is sedation. Will I be awake at all?

Carter the anesthesiologist comes in and explains the difference, Lila rising up and asking for specifics. I miss most of that. They turn to me.

I don't want to know of anything that happens, and yet, I would rather not puke. What's the best way to go? General is decided. I can see Lila not convinced, but as it is a brief procedure

71

and I won't be under long enough to really get sick from the drugs, she assents. OK. Good.

The medical team is now very concerned I go to the bathroom.

It is getting to be time, you need to go to the bathroom first.

Alright everybody, last call. $200 for coffee? Anybody? Jayne coos, I am taking you to the bathroom now. Leave your purse on the bed with Lila, anyway, we want to know where it is while you are in the bathroom cause of that $200.

Lila smiles and starts to collect my things.

> *Jesus Fucking Christ what if I die here? Well, I maybe won't*
> *die here, today,*
> *but if it is fucking cervical cancer I could die, here, on the*
> *east Coast, and I could die fast. I made them promise me out*
> *west they would not let me die on the east coast. They*
> *solemnly promised me. What will happen to him if I die? I*
> *should have gotten us both to California before now, where*
> *the bench is a little deeper, where he would have been taken*
> *care of. The bench here is Lila. Lila is the only bench.*

Lila the Bench picks up my purse.

Go ahead, Betty, she says, go with Jayne to the bathroom. They aren't making me leave yet.

Hooked up to the IV, I trail Jayne past the nurses' station to the bathroom. I pass my Doogie Howser in his scrubs. Jayne and I figure out some convoluted way for me, while hooked up to the pole, to use the toilet as she is outside the door holding a line and plastic bag of drugs aloft.

We, a slow train, rattle back to the bay. Lila has collected my things and is standing.

Betty, you are going in now. I'll be right outside. I was going for a walk, but now I'm not as this will be very quick, they tell me. They have my cell and they'll call me when you're out of surgery and they'll come for me when you wake up. It shouldn't be long.

It briefly flashes over me that I am lucky. Luck flashing, I'm transferred, wheeled into the operating room. Thank you, Lila.

I see, feel, hear, whirring around me; many people, many lights. Carter the anesthesiologist comes to me and talks to me about drugs. I see my doctor talking to nurses. I'm counting backwards. Then I see nothing.

Three voices above me are calling my name. Loudly, it seems. Why are all these people saying my name? Confused, I think I am upside down; I am topsy-turvy.

Oh, you're awake now! Great, we are wheeling you back to the bay. Everything went great.

Gruff June is waiting for me. Everything went great, I hear. I nod, I guess so. My doctor comes in and talks to me. I don't hear much except Everything Went Great. I try to shake off the anesthesia, like an Old English Sheepdog shaking off a sudden rainstorm in the back yard. Lila comes in.

Your doctor came out and talked to me while you were in recovery. He says it will be a week or so before the tests come back, but that he saw nothing, absolutely nothing, nothing, to indicate anything is seriously wrong and that you shouldn't worry anymore.

I don't have fucking cervical cancer???

Jayne says, back to the bathroom we go, you need to change and put this on. She is holding an Institutional Sparkle Pad. White, non-descript. I go with her to the bathroom, I take the Institutional Sparkle Pad from her and shut the door. As I start to take off the robe, I notice they have put a disposable panty on me, and I also notice that I am bleeding a lot. I peel down the disposable panty, find my real panties and tape up the hospital pad as best I can. Jesus Christ, that is what it must be like to be dead, and the undertaker dresses your body. You're unconscious as to be dead and some helpful nurse pulls some panties on you.

Dad, Larry and I have to be up at the funeral home at 2:00PM. Her body has just been brought in. They need to talk to us about the service, and they want us to bring clothes to bury her in.

I couldn't care less what we bury her in, and the thought of a 'service' makes me laugh. I shut my mouth, though, as my brother and I go through her clothes. We settle on

75

something, Larry babbles he wants her buried with this or that piece of jewelry the kids got her at one point I don't give a fuck just grab whatever you want and let's go I so don't give a fuck. I look at the bag of clothes Larry has pulled together. No underwear. I go back to her dresser and pull out a pair of panties. I remember telling the undertaker lady I can't have my mother buried with no underwear.

Through the door I call to Jayne. Is there supposed to be this much blood?

She comes in.

Yes, I know it looks bad, but you're OK.

Jayne leads the shuffle back to the bay. As we pass the nurse's station, I check in again with her.

Why does my vagina look like a Quentin Tarantino film?

I hear a guffaw from one of the nurses, who suddenly got very busy looking down at a chart she was holding.

Don't worry, the bleeding will stop soon. Make sure you take the Tylenol for pain. Should you need.

Gruff June and Lila are waiting by the bed. Jayne settles me in and gets me a blanket.

I'm bleeding like fuck, I whisper to Lila.

Don't worry, the bleeding will stop soon. Make sure you take the Tylenol for the pain. Should you need. Gruff June assures me, hearing from half a room away. She starts talking about her artist children who are coming to live with her. I, or Lila, must have told her I am an actor. I love that she has artist children, I tell her she is so lucky, artists are the best, I say, they give us life. Gruff June harrumphs, yes, it is a good thing that she has this stable nursing job now that the artists are coming, but I see her twinkle as she chats about them. We talk a little about acting. I look at these women around me. Lila arranges belongings. Jayne unhooks me from stuff. I look for my shoes.

I bow my head. Luck flashes.

Gruff June brings me coffee.

Terror Reads a Magazine

The thing about Alzheimer's is that you never know when Terror will leap out of a closet.

My father's morning routine is the same. I can hear from my room the first shamblings of awakeness from two doors down. He is sleeping later and later but I let that slide. (One of us is old and one of us is show folk; neither of us leap up to greet the dawn.) He will shuffle to the kitchen, a left at the couch. He will proceed to the table, get himself coffee, make toast. (He always leaves the buttery knife straight on the tablecloth; he had better not drink coffee out of my favorite mug. Irritates the shit out of me.) These things have been true, reliable things for two years.

This morning, shamble, shamble and I hear a right at the couch.

BOO!!! Terror blasts out of the closet.

I freeze at the desk. Terror slithers into my room and sits on my bed; a half-smile. I wait. The TV goes on (perpetually set at low volume, innocuous USA. I wonder if it is NCIS or SVU today). I wait, whiskers twitching. Terror cocks his head.

I move toward the kitchen. I look right, past the couch. Dad is sitting in his chair in front of the television (SVU). He looks fine, he looks the same.

Hi Dad.

Hi Dear.

Terror has followed me into the kitchen. No butter knife on the tablecloth. No "I Love NYC" mug on the table. Terror caresses my neck, icy claws freezing my throat. I swipe him off. I move back through the rooms, carefully not looking in Stabler's direction as I pass.

Sit down, collect yourself first. Drink some coffee (out of my favorite mug). Maybe he had gotten up earlier, already had coffee, maybe I just missed it. Calm down. You need to take ten minutes, drink your own coffee and get a grip before you find out what's up with this. Terror licks blood off his fangs and smiles warmly at me. He sits back down on the bed. I boot up the laptop, shakily.

When will I live in Paris? I better brush up my French. I search for Rosetta Stone.

Let me see NY job listings.

Fuck. The printer needs cartridges.

Terror flips through Better Homes and Gardens; eyes me, waits.

Let me check LA job listings. I am going to end up in LA anyway.

I sneak a glance at the cat. He is usually a great help in chasing away Terror, but these days he is so zonked up on the meds he makes Keith Richards look like a Bobbsey twin. No help there.

Now. Get Up. Deal. I put the empty favorite mug down. I walk to the couch and sit. Terror follows silently, but keeps a distance.

Hey Dad, are you feeling OK? You haven't had your coffee, or any toast.

Sure I did, I had it earlier. I just had some coffee. Yes, I feel fine, dear.

Terror snickers and advances on me, tongue out, panting. I side-step him.

Hmm, OK, well, we are going to get started on... (the other stuff, the other morning stuff that happens.) I will bring some coffee and an early lunch today, so let's get going on (the other morning stuff.)

He gets up. I take his arm, lead him haltingly into the bathroom. Everything checks out, his blood levels check out. I sit him back in front of Elliot. I go into the bathroom, shut the door and stay at the sink a very long time. Finally, I wipe the sink down from the puke, blood and tears. Washing my face, and before I start his lunch, I see that Terror, staved off for now, has tossed Better Homes and Gardens aside and slips back into the closet.

I notice a low light and feel the wintry draft through the slightly open door.

The Night Crew

I needed aides in the house

My night crew is a little crazier than my day crew. I think
that may be true in general of night crews, speaking as a creature of
the night, myself. We tend to be more off the grid, a tish more here
and there, back and forth, wilder at heart.

In a stable routine with the day shift, (Bella and Papa were a
great team) it was soon apparent we would need help at night, too,
especially as I travelled. Changing, dinner, meds, empty a pee
bucket: all fun evening activities that I could use a little help with.

Different agencies sent different people. They rotated, they
revolved, they talked a lot. They all wanted me to listen to their
vacation plans, their kid's vacation plans, their menus that night,

their home remedies. Most of them were experts on everything. One rattled on about how to put Depends on Papa without him actually having to take off his pants. I was working in the back room, dreading any encounter other than, Hi, yes, he is feeling pretty well tonight, we should be easy today, have at it…but at this little pronouncement I have to admit I opened one eye, unclenched an ass cheek and said, HUH? (Sure enough, it can be done.)

They came and went, they covered for Jane, who covered for Irene, who left the agency and went on vacation, had a baby, got married, divorced her dog and could only come on Tuesdays when her car was running.

Papa would look at me confusedly.

Her name is Rosa. The new agency called me and said she lived close by, she could come evenings, and also on the weekends twice a day (when I desperately needed help).

She is very young, early twenties, with a child at home (I gathered when I bothered to listen). I also vaguely picked up there was a husband in Another Country. Great, wonderful, don't care.

She would breeze in, often not in uniform but in some super summery shorty thing that I knew Dad probably didn't mind, so I let that slide. I let the erratic times slide, I let bringing a friend to sit in slide, I let things I didn't consider important slide. (I was a young girl once.) I knew she (and we) needed the gig, and she actually did a fine job when she was here. He liked her, she didn't talk much, in and out–terrific.

One week, though, she missed a couple of nights. I came home late and found a note. Dear Cate, your father is fine. I am sorry I missed Wednesday, I just found out my husband is cheating on me and I have pictures and I don't feel too good.

No, no, no, don't tell me, I don't want to know please don't tell me please just come in and wipe and smile and wear that summery thing and dole out pills and give him some nice ice tea and don't tell me and we don't care that you don't know that Depends trick and sweet fucking Jesus please God Jesus don't tell me.

She is very late the next evening, a beautiful June New England evening. The screen door is open, I am at the stove cooking dinner, Papa contentedly in the next room, watching something, it doesn't really matter anymore what, but he seems happy waiting for his dinner.

She comes in and stands at the kitchen table, looking down, pulling on gloves. She asks me, Did you get my note?

Yes, Rosa, and I am so sorry to hear that, must be very tough for you right now. Not fully turning from the stove, please fucking Jesus God don't tell me, my head is going to blow right off if I hear anything at all not pertaining to my immediate deal, you're not going to tell me are you?

I stir and stir. Silence. I turn around. She is standing in the same place, plastic gloves on, looking down as one tear drop slips, then another, then a million.

Rosa, sit down, let me get you some water. Do you want some lemon in it? When did you find out? Did your friend in Another Country confront him? How is the baby? Terrible, what the hell are they thinking?

Daddy, Rosa and I are talking a bit in the kitchen, are you OK for a little while until dinner?

Oh, sure, honey.

I mean, we're all just slogging through it, right? Together.

Dr. Hoffman Asks Me a Question

Managing the aides is a full time job on its own. At one point, during full-on Aides Palooza, there were people in the house for two hours a day in the morning and two hours a day in the evening, seven days a week. Until we settled on a somewhat stable crew it was very disorienting for both my father and myself, all these folks telling us what to do. For the most part, they were very helpful taking care of my father's personal needs. However, our schedules weren't our own, and I could see how this tired him. Some of the bad aides were truly disturbing.

Diamond Lil showed up at the house one day. Aides are supposed to report for duty in uniform, scrubs. I'm not much of a stickler for these types of rules. I usually don't care what they're wearing as long as he is happy, changed, pilled and fed. However, Diamond Lil had her best cashmere on and was dripping in, well, diamonds. Every finger had multiple sparkly rings, her arms were bedazzled in bracelets, expensive earrings cascaded from shrew ears.

Concerned, I say a nicer version of, Umm, Diamond Lil, your hands are soon to be full of Fixodent and poopy, you might maybe wanna de-jewel for your tour of duty here.

Oh no, she wouldn't de-jewel and didn't like wearing scrubs.

Uh huh.

She voiced a couple of horrified thoughts at the state of the house, and also had some commentary on my role here.

I say a nicer version of, Um, Diamond Lil, you think I don't know this lean-to is a shithole? You think I don't see that ceiling falling in? You think I don't know I won't be able to beat back all these spiders crawling up my ass? I got this covered, Diamond Lil, and I am here to get him out as soon as possible. I sure don't need your insightful observations, though, so shut it and go wipe something.

Diamond Lil did not last long.

One of the social workers mentions I should look into the adult foster care program. Adult foster care is a state program wherein the client is placed in my care. Round the clock tending, all food, meds, doctor appointments, bill paying, shopping, home maintenance, can all be done by the foster care person. Can all be done by me.

I think about this. This would solve-ish two problems. One being my father and myself would have some semblance of normal life back without all those people in and out. The other is money. There is a small daily stipend paid to the caregiver through the AFC. Hardly enough to make much of a difference, but something. I left my job last year and my unemployment ran out six months ago.

Of course, I always thought, I will be able to get a part-time Betty Secretary job at the local tool and die up here in the woods. I was applying and interviewing since the day I left the New York job. Not a nibble, not one. Oh, I'd get called in. Some of the more ridiculous interviews were second rounders in front of a panel of four or five people all grilling me for what was essentially a gussied up coffee-getter.

I have no illusions. I AM a gussied up coffee-getter; an actor, writer who always had a day job. I stayed at those day jobs in Los Angeles and New York for long periods of time as I usually loved the jobs and the people that came along with those jobs. I had one betty interview me on the phone and flat out tell me, no, I am not appropriate for this coffee-getter position because it was all about the getting of the coffee. She said, You'd basically be my secretary and you have far more experience for this type of thing. Aim higher, she said. Aim higher? All I am looking for is to park a mug in front of you terribly busy execs and hightail it back to the house (because God knows what will happen in the four or five hours I am away). I appreciated her honesty, even though I certainly didn't want to aim higher. Most of the others, I suspect have more to do with being a 58-year-old woman in America. Don't be a 58-year-old woman in America. Just don't. Let me write that down somewhere.

I am a 58-year-old woman in America. I wasn't always a 58-year-old woman in America. I had day jobs, but I lived for art. Making art, seeing art, hearing art. My community was artists and health care workers. I put the phone down from the Aim Higher betty and knew it was over. I am not going to get hired here, or, probably anywhere, ever again. I angrily let that sink in. Taking care of my elderly, demented father will now be my day job. (Don't die, Daddy, that will be the ultimate down-sizing for me.)

I wonder if it will be too much for me to handle.

I was doing much of the Dad maintenance anyway, but was not looking forward to the personal care, the showers, the diaper changing that the aides now had full responsibility for. My father didn't bargain for any of this either.

I call the Adult Foster Care people. I fill out mountains of paperwork. I talk to endless people on the phone. I sit through three or four site visits. Jesus, I have fix up this hellhole so it looks livable. I have to find those carbon dioxide/smoke alarm things, a fire extinguisher. Get him one of the clothes closet things for his room. Up to now we've been sharing a wardrobe in the front room, but regs dictate he needs all this bullshit in his own room. I bought this huge thing, it is a third of the size of the room, and he only has four shirts. Neither he nor I have many clothes. He hasn't bothered for some time and I have just now stopped bothering. After all this stuff is loaded in, I have the last site visit. The social worker and nurse come in, check off boxes and we're set. Well, set is perhaps not the word for it, but, we are on our own.

Is this more than I can handle?

We slog through the day to day, eventually finding a rhythm that sort of works. Sometimes. I take that as a win. Except when I lose.

I placed dad in temporary respite care as I attend a wedding reception in Michigan. As explained by the Veterans Association, I can place Dad in a nursing home for however many days a year if I am travelling, so I do this for this trip.

I get a call when I am out of town. Dad has fallen in the nursing facility. When I pick him up two days later, he cannot walk. I am incredulous. Before I realize the severity of the injury, before I see he can't even stand up, I call him a drama queen.

Dad, we gotta go, I've packed your stuff up, just stand up out of the chair and let's get moving. He mewled, tried to stand and fell back into the chair.

Dad, stop being such a drama queen, let's go. I throw that over my shoulder as I am grabbing something off his bedside table.

I called my father a drama queen.

I barely contain my fury as it takes three attendants to load him into the pickup. Dad is in extreme pain as I drive him over to the nearest emergency room, one town over from us. I am trying to still the whirling volcano inside me, if only to outwardly stay calm. Why the hell am I driving this old man from a nursing home that I placed him in for RESPITE care, directly to a fucking emergency room? I asked that very question to the three Shady Rest attendants as they hoisted a howling old man into the passenger seat.

I have to take my father directly to an emergency room because he leaves your facility unable to walk. I really don't know what else to do, but you can see the hell in that, right?

The three silent stricken faces looked up at me. Somebody mumbled something about sorry.

Yeah, I am fucking sorry too, I have to take him to the ER dad do you think you can walk no I don't I shouldn't have been released from there do you think I don't know dad I don't know what their deal is but if you can't walk we're fucked we are going over to the ER ok dear whatever you think yeah I think.

I pull into the parking lot (yay for that handicap placard we just got), leave him in the truck and I flounder to the desk. They sense I am in a fair amount of trouble and an attendant quickly brushes aside my jumbled "I can drive him around to the entrance and we can get him down from there" attempt to be helpful.

No, no, I will go out to the truck, where are you parked?

In one of the handicap (yay, placard) spots, close.

He brings a wheelchair and helps dad down. We wheel into an ER exam room. Dad is transferred to a bed. Nurses, admission people teem around us. Someone brings him a blanket. He is cold. He is always cold. I recite what happened forty times. I sign forty things. I pull an ID for him. I babble I can sign for him; he is in my foster care.

What's that, someone says? I don't really know the answer, other than he is in my care. That's what I say, he is in my care., like a foster kid, only he is 86. I look over at Dad. He's cold. He's shivering. He looks like hell, really.

I had to leave him in that place, to go to a wedding. Don't think about that. You didn't know. Anything can happen at any time. It's not your fault.

I look down at my father. He's cold, but now drifting off to sleep in the ER.

I first spot him through the ER doors. Oh yeah, that's the ER doc. I forgot he might be here, what was his name again? He reminds me of someone. A handful, trouble. He looks like the type of man that maybe got into some trouble in Reno, maybe or maybe not she was alive when he left the hotel room and now he is banished to a small town ER. That kind of trouble. What was his name again? He comes through the double doors.

How are we?

Living the dream, I say. He smiles. I tell him what happened (forty-first). He turns to Dad, does it hurt here? There? Ok, we'll take x-rays. Ok, I say, thanks Dr. (I get the first partial glimpse of his badge, Samuel) Dr. Samuel. He stops and smiles again at me. He actually pulled some stitches out of me at one point last year, pulled stitches out, admitted me, transferred me. He has seen a couple of things of mine already. I know he doesn't remember, but I do. A friend and I would later compete over who Dr. Samuel got more intimate with. Oh sure, Betty, you just had to go the emergency room for that sprain, and you just had to tell me how his hand lingered a few minutes longer than necessary on your shoulder. I couldn't compete with that and was less than graceful about it.

We wait. Vitals taken, insurance verified, X-rays, Dr. Samuel comes back. Now I see the whole badge (his first-name is Samuel last-name Hoffman). Dr. Hoffman says to me, it's a small pelvic fracture, that's why he is in so much pain. He won't be able to put any weight on his right side for a while. He won't need surgery, though. He stops. He looks down at his clipboard. I, on the other side of the bed, look at Dr. Hoffman. Dr. Hoffman asks, without looking up, I think...is this more than you can handle?

I can't handle any of this fucking bullshit, Dr. Hoffman. Zero things can I handle here. Will you marry me, Dr. Hoffman? Can we walk out of here right now? Can somebody pick up this shift for you? Do you live close by, Dr. Hoffman? Can we go to dinner maybe? I am feeling like I could love some mussels marinara? Do you like seafood, Dr. Hoffman? Maybe after dinner we can quietly walk back to the house and sit on the couch. We don't need to talk, that's nice when you are with someone that you don't have to talk with isn't it, Dr. Hoffman? I had a boyfriend once, Dr. Hoffman. Before the husband, before I was wrecked, before the other one. He was really the best boyfriend. We lived on the lower east side, east 12th street. We had an apartment together for four or five years. He

97

was kind. We cooked together, we had our friends over. We cooked soft shelled crabs for our friends. It was a small apartment, but I remember that couch we had, green and gold. He worked at a restaurant and got home late. I would nap on the couch waiting for him to come home. I remember this one particular nap, it was a wintery night, I set the lights low, I had the radio on WNEW, that was our favorite. I remember that specific nap as the most peaceful time in my entire life, that night dropping off to sleep waiting for my boyfriend to come home, knowing he was on his way home to see me. Do you have a green and gold couch, Dr. Hoffman? Well, no matter, the color. Do you think I could lie down on the couch when we get home? You could sit by me, maybe read a book, maybe talk softly about that hotel thing. I'll listen. We're all broken, Dr. Hoffman. Did you know that the Japanese repair their broken ceramics by painting over the cracks with gold so you can see the beauty of the imperfections? I would love to see that sometime. We don't need to talk, though, you can go back to reading, and I will drop off. Wouldn't that be a peaceful thing, Dr. Hoffman? We will be easy; we will be slow.

He looks up from the clipboard, across the bed. Across my father who is nearly all gone. I nod. He nods back at me. I will arrange for him to go straight into rehab for a couple of weeks, he says. I don't say anything. I nod. He nods again. He doesn't look at me. He leaves.

A herd of nurses clops in.

The doctor is sending your dad to rehab. We will contact This One and then we will contact That One if This One can't take you today. If you don't get into either today, Dr. Hoffman is admitting your father into the hospital anyway and we will get him into This One or That One tomorrow.

I didn't see Dr. Hoffman again. I drove home alone and put my head down for a while.

The Piss Load

Old people stink.

He was home from rehab for three days. A rocky three days. He wasn't well. This was a turning point. I kept trying to make it not a turning point. Hey, Dad, let's do that Ordinary Thing we always do, wanna do that now? He looks blankly, meekly attempts the Ordinary Thing, but pain, fatigue, fragility defeats most Ordinary Things in the end.

I keep him stationary. I pick up the slack around Ordinary Things not being done. One of the Ordinary Things is the bathroom. He can't make it to the bathroom, and he is especially incontinent overnight. Clothes, sheets, blankets all need to be washed. He broke our washing machine last year (that's right, Cathy, blame the

Alzheimer's patient for breaking the equipment. I have to make the point he broke it. He should have not shaken it so hard, he never took care of anything here…he never took care of me).

Everything smelled like piss. I couldn't walk into the bathroom without retching. I piled pissy blankets, pissy chucks, pissy clothes into the broken washer, now merely a hamper.

Not my things, though. No, not my finery. Up till now, I took the laundry to the laundromat every week and washed our clothes together. Not now, let's see, do I shove everything into a garbage bag and haul it like that? Easier, as I can drag it on the ground and get it through the door faster. Easier that way so the goddamn cat has less of a chance to escape. I can shimmy a little faster out the door dragging a bag.

I open the washer-now-a-hamper and am knocked back by the fumes of piss. No. No. Separate washes. I pull gloves on and shove clothes into two separate garbage bags (Piss and Non Piss). I throw in an off-brand detergent. Now thoroughly unnerved, I pull the two bags out the door.

Cheddar indeed escapes, darting away as I fumble with the door. The wretched little thing easily outruns me for a while.

Chasing him, the day is already collapsing around me. The laundry, shopping, his meds and lunch, meet with a nurse, a social worker, someone, I forget who. An evening meeting for a local town committee that I don't really have the time for, yet I committed, sister. Him. My fading chances. I am not going to make it out of here, am I?

Cheddar slows and bends halfway around a fence. This is a true break, as he is so concentrated on his big game he doesn't feel my approach, even though I was awhirl with the day carousel-ing around me. I mean, how dumb are you, cat, you don't feel me and my tornado closing in on you? I grab his tail and snatch him up. Yowling, he nevertheless lets me carry him back inside. His mistake is to assume he was free.

Dad, I am going to do laundry. This time, he asks me if he can help. Can I help with anything, dear? Maybe I can do something. (No, no, you just sit there and wait for me. If you can manage not to piss your pants, actually that would be helpful. You could die, that would be even more helpful, wouldn't it?)

No, I will be back soon, and then I will fix you some lunch.

I throw the two bulging garbage bags into the back of the pick-up. I throw the off-brand detergent after, hoping it lands somewhere in the back. No pretty fabric softener or nice dryer sheets.

I collapse over the steering wheel. Eventually I pull my face off the wheel, start the truck and head uptown.

I see her about town. I named her Sally. I don't know what her name is. I call her Sally. She pushes her laundry cart around, rain or shine. She talks to herself. She shakes a bit. I asked around about her. Oh, yes, someone always clucks sympathetically. Schizophrenic, mental problems. A shame, really. Nobody seems to know where she lives. I heard one time, maybe a group home. Sally is always moving. I never see her at rest. She pushes the cart ferociously, urgently going somewhere, anywhere.

I wish I had Sally's laundry cart. (I am this close to being Sally.) I am dragging these clothes in a garbage bag whereas if I had a laundry cart like Sally I would be a little less likely to fall off the world. (I am Sally.)

Hi, fellow washers at the Fluffy Fold. Oh, here we all are, must be a Tuesday morning again! See me here with my sparkly laundry cart (cost a fortune at Target). I am certainly not dragging a bunch of panties around in an old Hefty, now, am I? No siree, no living on the edge here, no hanging on for dear life here with this state-of-the art, respectable, proper laundry cart. Let's see, I also tucked in the fabric softener and dryer things that go in the dryer to make everything smell nice.

(Hi fellow Fluffy Folders! Can we all pretend you don't see me this week? I am dragging two Heftys and I don't have the softener or dryer sheets. Please ignore my shaking because I caught myself actually wondering when my father was going to die and free me from this Piss Load right here. My hair isn't washed and I don't remember the last time I had a shower. Heh heh, yeah, you're right, I should just pour some (off-brand) detergent on my head and shove myself into a third machine, aren't you the witty one this week?)

I load up my elegant finery into one machine. I turn to the Piss Load. Fuck, I should have brought my gloves.

Something clatters to the floor. I was blown backward as if by a bomb blast. I look down. A grimy, somewhat toothless Ace pocket comb had dropped.

He always kept a comb in his pocket. This was a man who liked to comb his hair, who liked to look nice. This was a man who was tall and handsome. This was a man who liked his wallet in his back pocket. I had taken it out weeks ago. I think it was on the kitchen table. A while ago I had even stopped slipping a twenty in. He has stopped being anxious if he doesn't have any cash on him. This was a man who always knew when it was time for a haircut.

I crashed down on one of the unsteady white plastic chairs that lined the walls, transfixed by the harmless plastic black comb on the floor. I start to shake badly. I manage to walk to the comb and pick it up off the floor. I tuck it into my purse. Choking, I check the rest of the clothes for combs, wallets or other such talismans and then put the second load in a machine.

It was September 5th, 1980 something. Early 80's, I think. Maybe 1982. Yes, then. I was married for four years, so that makes me being not married in 1986. The year of the Mets. That's how I remember it, not being married for that World Series. However, on the morning of that happy September day in 1982 (I think), I was about to be married. The light was a golden wash, the light I always

105

imagined California was bathed in. The gold I always saw

Steinbeck's Salinas in. The soft gold light poured through an open

side door of the rectory where my father and I waited to be called,

cued. The shafts were alive as dust particles danced through the

gold. I shivered in my strapless gown on that morning in

Washington Heights. I wanted to be inside that shimmering honey

gold; wanted it to warm me. I could hear friends and family coming

into to the small, Episcopal church. Well, friends. No family. My

father was the only family member who attended my wedding. He

was there, sitting with me that morning, looking at the gold rush in

that side door.

The door opened onto a side street, 177th St. We sat and

watched Washington Heights go about its day, ever listening to my

friends and my soon-to-be husband's family and friends enter the

church. Dad looked good, John had loaned him some clothes. He

tucked a comb in his pocket. I was in a ridiculously meringue-y long

dress, with a ridiculously long train, and even longer veil. (The train

would get down the aisle twenty minutes after I would.) As

showtime neared, my father looks at me, then nods to the open side

door.

You know, he says, we could just go down to the diner there and get a cup of coffee.

What? I say. Huh?

Well, if you wanted to do that, instead. We could just walk out the door, here (through the gold) and go on down to that diner on the corner, maybe get coffee instead of this. It would be OK.

I gather the meringue about me, fold it over, wrap it around me several times. I unpin the veil and train. I leave them on Father Paul's desk. I stand. My father stands, steps back and gestures to the open doorway. I step down into the street. Dad follows. A gust of wind blows up, partially unwrapping me. Leaves are caught in the silk; we shake them loose and start down the street. We pass the video store. Not open yet, but I think maybe on the way back we can rent a movie for later. The diner is a small storefront, this side of dingy. We push open the door. The bell rings. I smell coffee. We walk towards the counter and I re-wrap myself over one of the stools, my father sits next to me. Eggs, yes, and toast. Oatmeal, Dad, you'll have that? Yes, two coffees. Thanks. Just cream for both of us. Remind me to pick up a paper for later. Do you want tomato juice? I think I will. Could I have a lemon wedge with that?

I don't know, I picked up that habit somewhere; it makes it tangier.
I also salt down my tomato juice pretty good, too. I never had a
sweet tooth. It was always salt for me. Remember when I would
read a book as a kid I would eat a jar of pickles, and then drink all
the pickle juice, too? He laughs, nods.

No, Dad, I am alright. It's OK. It will be OK.

Ok.

We hear music; someone fetches us and we head in. I turn
my head and watch as the side door closes.

I leave the laundry mat and walk back to the truck. I sit there
awhile and wonder how it works: who gets to forgive whom?

Un-absolved, I stop shaking enough to start the engine. I am
already late for all this other stuff happening today. I can do the
shopping while the wash goes.

On the way to the store, I swing by the barber's to double-
check the hours.

Why Do Everybody Else's Parents Get To Die?

Oh, no, Bella, I'm so sorry. Your grandma? Oh no, when was this? Sunday? How old was she? Eighty-four?

Eighty-four? I tried very hard to keep the unabashed envy out of my voice.

OH MY GOD!!! You are so lucky!!! She died just now?? When? How, what happened? WOW, that was fast? WOW, so now it's over for you guys, huh? Your mom doesn't have to go over there every day. You don't have to fight with her every day... stop smoking, it'll kill ya, stop making me do all this stuff, stop bossing me around, stop being so fussy about going shopping. Oh wow, Bella, I am so happy for you! Jesus, I am so screwed with him and here's a little secret nobody tells you, these fucking old people aren't worth it. They're stupid and they're selfish and they're awful and they need shit like, 24/7. 24 fucking 7, my friend, I kid you not. And you just got SPRUNG. You lucky bitch, you just hit the mother load in the roulette spin of Will My Elderly Family Members Live Forever and Fuck Me? game. Wow! Ding ding ding… come on down!!

God, he is eighty-six. How the jumping hell is he still alive? How is he still going? Bella's granny just dropped at eighty-four. I mean, c'mon, it's hardly fair to me. Granny wasn't even at the place where she needed all this bullshit yet. I mean, sure, maybe Mommy the daughter would check on her, take her shopping, whatever. But I don't think it was the full-on deal: cooking, bill-paying, certainly not ass-wiping. Maybe it was getting close. Granny just got out of the hospital, Mommy was going over there more and more, I guess. But still. Granny was living alone. And this dying thing came quickly for Granny, a shocker. I feel badly for Bella because they seem rather unprepared for it. And they seem kinda sad about it, I am sorry for them, somewhat, but at eighty-four, a quick stroke, or whatever it was, done and done. You'll get through the shock. But how lucky can you be? I am envious of my friends with quick-dying parents and grandparents. No endless caretaking, meds, food preparation. No upended lives, no living in poverty in shacks in the woods, no piss smells wafting, hanging; especially in summer. No endless re-explaining who everybody is. No un-ending stretches of hating yourself, wondering, waiting for him to die. Waiting for your own life to resume.

Dad, get up, it's time for me to take you to the doctor's.

I am stopping by the rest home where I have placed him in respite care while I travel to New York.

Dad, we are just going to run up the road; your doctor is very close to here, where you are staying. I went to New York, Dad, I'm back a day to work a bit. I have to turn around tomorrow and go back on the road, and then Sunday you are coming back home.

Oh, he says. Well, that's good.

He is in bed. It is a single bed. He is covered with a blanket. He is half asleep when I come in. Goddamn it, I told them three times I was coming at 3:00. We only have a half hour to get him to the appointment. I really was expecting him up, dressed, sitting in his chair waiting for me. While I didn't quite expect him to be painting a landscape, or cracking the atom, or delving into Proust while he was waiting, I DID expect him to be at least, vertical.

OK, Dad, we gotta get moving. I am raising the bed so you can sit and get up. He takes off his covers and struggles up.

He is grayer, older, frailer than when I left him five days before. I notice he looks different. I also notice he is not tethered to the bed. I was quite insistent in the run-up to this visit that he be alarmed-up. An alarm should be affixed to him so that when he rises to walk anywhere, the nurse's station is notified to assist him to the bathroom. He had previously fallen in another facility. His frailness and disorientation make him a very high fall risk and I was concerned when I left him. I take note to speak to the nurse when we get back about securing him to the bed or chair.

Please don't leave me. Please don't leave me all alone in the world. I am terrified of being alone. It will frighten me to death, it really will. All my yelling about being alone, well....

I want to say, just get better, just stop getting worse. Can't you try to remember things more? Do you remember up in Maine, you bought Larry and I cherry popsicles? I didn't like cherry and ground mine down the bathroom sink. Larry caught me and said we better not tell you. I remember when you bought them, at that little store in town. I remember you hesitating at the counter, like maybe wondering if you could afford the popsicles. I always wanted to say thank you for that popsicle and that now cherry is my favorite flavor.

Can you not ache all over? Can you just not do that? Can you just feel better? Can you feel spryer? I want you to walk quickly beside me. I want to dance on your shoes again. Can we play chess again? Can you be the boss of things again? I don't want to be the boss of things anymore. I'm not smart enough. I'm not strong enough. I really am cowardly. I really don't have it in me.

You're not going to leave me here, are you? All alone? That's not the plan, is it?

How do you feel, Dad? We really do have to get moving. He is slow to move, to stand. Jesus Christ, you have to move faster, we are running a little late and I thought you were going to be ready and you're not ready.

We stop by the nurse's station. I am checking him out to go to the doctor. Oh wait, they say, there is paperwork. We didn't know he was going today, he needs to take this paperwork to the doctor, his meds, etc. Well, can you pull that together a little faster?

(I told you guys last week that today I was coming in to… oh fuck it, just hurry the hell up can you hurry up this is hell enough).

We stagger to the pickup. He actually moves faster than I do. He is frail and in danger of falling, but he is faster than I. Yeah, I do need to lose that 100 pounds and get back to physical therapy. Fuck, he will fucking live forever and I could die tomorrow. My goddamn luck.

An aide, Tony, takes us from the waiting room. He leads us down the hallway, jauntily. Tony is friendly, be-bopping down the hall. He talks to Dad, taking his weight, vitals. He calls him young man (patronizing, I know) but still asks about his hat. Dad talks to him. I spit out the requisite Alzheimer's and deaf that I upchuck to all new people dealing with him. Oh, and he calls everybody babe, don't be offended. Tony laughs, and turns to Dad and takes his blood pressure. Roll up your sleeve, young man. I suddenly start to tear up, unable to stop from crying. I look around the room. White, everything is white. I also see metal, a little of silver metal instruments. I study them. The room has the shabby, neglected, overused and understaffed feel to it that most poor-people-hospitals do. Tony had mentioned he was working a double and somebody called out sick. I turn to study the tongue depressors so they don't see me cry a little. I think I cry because here is a precious ten minutes when he is somebody else's responsibility, not mine, and I am grateful for the ten minutes. I think I cry for all of us, poor, in that room with Tony on his double shift, be-bopping up blood pressures on old veterans, that's what I think, anyway. I think those things.

What are you doing? I ask. He looks up. He has parts of his new electric razor all over his lap. Dad, what are you doing? It doesn't work, it doesn't work, he says, shaking his head. Well, Dad, you can't take it apart like that. What's the matter, why isn't it working? He looks at me, confused. I don't know, it isn't working. Irritated, I take it from him. I piece it together as best I can, not being handy at these things, myself. OK, well, try it now. Oh, yes, that's OK now. Can you remember why you took it apart in the first place? No, it just wasn't working.

I got it for him last year for Father's Day. Speaking of not working, I wasn't myself, last year and only spent about twenty-five dollars on it. Well, Dad, Father's Day is coming up, I will get you a better one. How about that? Oh, yes, that's good, OK. So, can you limp though with this one for a while? Oh yes, I think so. I noticed he had it plugged in, maybe there was something with the charging, that was wonky. Well, ha, we were working this year so I'll get him a big fancy electric razor this Father's Day. What a good daughter I am! Oh yes, no worries, Old Sir, soon you will have the finest razor in the land. One so fine and grand all you will have to do is sit there like a king and it will shave you itself. You won't have to lift a finger, it will be so grand fancy fine it will shave you, while showing you pictures of the grandchildren (who never visit) and laughing and telling tales of the old days to you. You will never have to take it apart to figure out why it isn't running because everything is my fault for not being a better daughter and I will have a little more money to spend on the grand fancy fine one this year. Don't you worry one bit, motherfucker – to steal a David Sedaris bit from *You Can't Kill the Rooster*.

Give it to me. You broke it? You broke the new one? What's the matter with you? These are expensive, you know. Why do you keep breaking them? This is the second one. My voice rises, high, shrieky. I don't recognize my voice. Why do you keep taking them apart? Why do you keep breaking them? Higher, shriekier. He looks at me. I see the distress in his eyes. I don't know, he says. He says it again, I don't know.

Well, I say, as I snatch the pieces from him, look at this, I can't put this back together again. I sort of try to piece the razor back. No, you see. I can't put it back together. This one is ruined, too. You ruined it (in my like-I-have-a-cocker-spaniel voice). We have to throw this one away now (bad dog). I make a show of throwing the pieces in a nearby trash can. I make too much of a show of it. I catch myself.

I draw a deep breath and sit down. You know, maybe we are better off if I get you a better manual shaver, and some nice shaving cream. Wouldn't that be a little easier, do you think? (Good dog, Mommy's sorry, here do you want a treat?) Oh yes, he said, that would be better. Yes, I think so, I said, I will do that tomorrow, I will get a razor and shaving cream and then we can shave after your shower. I will help you. (Here, Mommy got you a new brush, let's brush that pretty coat.) Oh, OK, that's good.

I change and pill him. I bring dinner, and slip in some extra fruit.

Fiddleheads and Ambrosia Salad

I could see her down the long hall, mopping her way towards me. I sat in a walled in, glass office. My door was slightly ajar. It was morning, not early, but I was the first one in. The window was open, and the breeze of mid-December blew in.

What was her name? Joanie? Cheryl? She mopped closer and closer, nearing my end of the hall. She was thin and had blond-gray hair, she wore a bright green t-shirt and black pants. She pushed the mop back and forth the shiny lacquered floor, close enough to see me now. She nods hello. I nod back, through the glass walls of my office. I get up to open my door further.

What was it my supervisor, Alma, told me last night? Something about her, something about a run-in she had with the

119

others down at the other end of the hall. Administration lived at the other end and they could be a mean bunch. My group down here was much more benign. Alma and Debbie (that was her name, Debbie) talked last night, and Debbie said Administration complained about her, and her managers in housekeeping reprimanded her.

Debbie arrives at my open door, mop in hand, and knocks timidly.

Debbie, of course you can come in, you don't need to knock, I'm just getting settled in this morning. It's pretty clean, maybe just a quick run over the floor. How are you doing, Debbie? Everything OK, all set for the holidays? She shrugs, well, it won't be too much this year. You heard what happened yesterday? I say I didn't (Alma cautioned me against mentioning the incident if I saw Debbie). Well, she says, I was down the other end of the hall, she jerks her head resentfully in that direction. I was just mopping the offices down there and the door was open and I went in and started cleaning. I saw she (Lady Head Administrator) was on the phone, but I was going to be quick. Anyway, I go in her office just to clean the office, I was real quick and it only took a couple minutes. Later that morning my supervisor called me and said they complained about me. Now I need to do those offices last. Now I need to start in another building and work my way over here. She shook her head. I shook my head.

I picked up my coffee and opened my string cheese. I shook my head again. I switched gears. What are you doing for the holidays? I asked. Anything special? Oh, well, we are doing an office party next week, she said. Oh, I say brightly, where? Is the department throwing you guys something? She snorted. No, we all bring something. She said it would be over in facilities; a part of the college I never go to.

We are all waiting to see if we get a raise, she said. We find out next week, right around the time of the party. Oh, you guys are paid differently than we are. I guess it's different when you're salaried. We are hourly so it's probably very different than what you and they get (jerks her head resentfully down the hall again). I don't know, I said. I didn't know. I had been there only a few months, myself. She pushed the mop around my floor. You are all nicer to me than (another jerk of the head). I always like coming down here and talking to the people on this end of the hall. They aren't so nice down there. I wonder if we will get that raise, she wondered again. It won't be much, but it will help some. She mopped under the conference table.

Debbie, what are you bringing to the holiday party? I ask after a while. Oh I don't know yet, she says, maybe meatballs. MMMMM, I say. What do other people bring? Well, she says, the Spanish girl will bring that rice dish. Oh, I say, paella? I LOVE paella. She shakes her head. I don't know what it's called, but it has rice and some sort of pork in it. Maybe olives. She brought it last year. Some people liked it. It's different, she says. Oh, I say, I used to live in New York City and my Puerto Rican friends would make me the most wonderful rice dish, and I forget what it's called, too, Debbie. But it was this great yellow rice. I had never seen rice that yellow before, with smoked pork, yes! My friend's mother slow cooked that pork all day. They used all these spices I had never tasted before. And there were little peas in it too. I never had anything like that before. I loved it. Yes, she says, it is something like that. Some people had to get used to it. I liked it, I guess. Anyway, she will bring that. Yeah, I liked it I guess. The party will be right around the time we hear whether we'll get a raise, so I hope the mood of the party will be good.

She mops around the cabinet (where she has already mopped). Yeah, she says again, I liked it alright, the Spanish girl's rice.

New York Food

I'll go to Arthur Avenue to pick up clams, I say. You guys go to the theatre and I will cook here so dinner will be ready when you get back. It was New Year's Eve. My friend Jennie and her husband Jim were in from LA visiting her mom, Margaret. Margaret lived in a large, only in your dreams, apartment on west 83rd street, right off Broadway. She got tickets to War Horse that night for them, and Jennie had asked me over for dinner afterwards. Go ahead, I'll cook, I say. I have been cooking a lot lately and I have been playing with Clams con le Vongole. Clams in a garlic, white wine sauce. I can make that, it's quick, and we can have bread and a salad. All of us loved seafood. We had a few great pilgrimages to the Oyster Bar in Grand Central.

Half the fun of Clams con le Vongole was going to Arthur Avenue in the Bronx for the clams. The street was all red and green with Christmas and Italian flags, and the old Italian markets and restaurants were jam-packed. As I grabbed some fresh littlenecks, I spotted a Soprano talking to the Mike's Deli guys. I wandered around a bit, sat for an espresso, and headed back to 83rd street. Everybody kissed, we toasted the day, and they flounced out to the theatre.

Alone in Margaret's splendid kitchen, I sat on the cushioned wrap around settee. The bench wrapped around the table, so you had to slide in, around it. The kitchen settled around me like a fuzzy blanket. I sat in the quiet.

It was not usually quiet around that table. Jennie would fly in from LA to see her mother. She and I would talk and catch up, while she cooked. Margaret had a TV in the kitchen, so sometimes we would watch Top Chef and yap about food. Margaret and Jennie were watchful over me, especially in the later years as I struggled with back problems. They clucked and fussed as I limped in. They would lead me directly to the table, where I slid around as best I could. Wine was opened, a cheese tray assembled.

Now, alone, at the table, I was happy and full of thoughts of my friends, out in the New York City night, out in the lights, soon to come home to me while I cooked for them.

It was a Tyler Florence recipe. Boil the water for pasta. Throw linguini in for eight to ten minutes, until al dente. It had to be linguini, not spaghetti or angel hair. Meanwhile, scrub the clams and rinse. In a sauce pan, heat olive oil, then add garlic and red pepper flakes. Add the clams, wine and lemon juice. Cover until the clams open, about seven minutes. Here I also added a can of chopped clams (unlike Tyler). Add the hot, drained pasta, along with butter to the pan. Season with salt and pepper and sprinkle with fresh, chopped parsley.

I heard the door open. Is dinner ready? We're starving. Come in, come in, yes almost. They troop into the kitchen. MMMMM, it smells great! Jennie opens wine. And War Horse? Incredible, right? Those puppets, they say. Oh yes, I say, I sobbed like a little girl through most of it, ha! Those puppets, right?

The hot Clams von le Vongole was brought to the table. Jennie brought out a salad and a long baguette. We slid across the bench around the table. Midnight and champagne.

Happy New Year, my friends.

Food Here

I'd been looking for them at the market for a couple of weeks now. It was spring, May, and they were only in season for 45 minutes a year, it seemed. We missed them last year; we must have blinked. Fiddleheads. Little, green, pre-ferns. Fiddleheads are a New England thing, I believe. Harvested in spring, they were found mainly around wetlands, rivers, in only a two to three-week period in springtime. They were always a treat for the family. Dad loved them. In the early years here, my mother and a Euell Gibbons-type friend of hers (she was er, eccentric, and had eccentric friends) would forage for them down by the river.

Dad would dish them out, and he and I and my mother and brother would pounce on them. There would usually be something else trotted out for dinner, mainly for show, mainly ignored. The four of us, for an hour each spring, gathered around the table in harmony and peace thanks to a little green fern.

We hadn't foraged in many a year, and this year I was determined not to miss my window at the market. Then one day, there they were! First thing as you walk in, a big pile of mossy, gleaming, shiny, tiny, coiled ferns. I grabbed a plastic bag and dove into the heap.

How do you cook them? Someone asked me.

Well, we always just boiled the shit out of them, I say. Salt and pepper and butter. We didn't like them on the al dente side. You also had to douse them in cider vinegar. They needed a lot of acid. Some years I tried lemon, and one year I had the audacity to try balsamic vinegar. In town for a visit from New York City, where I was living, the Balsamic Vinegar Experiment was quickly condemned as I was assailed as the fancy, elitist, know-it-all, Democratic, commie, socialist, what's-the-matter-ain't-cider-vinegar-good-enough-for-ya food snob from the City. Yup, OK, cider vinegar it is. The same thing happened when I steamed fresh broccoli, instead of serving packaged frozen broccoli boiled so thoroughly it was practically pureed. Around the table that night, there were no takers for the crunchy vegetable. I remember being a little angry. Won't these hicks try anything new? This revealing my food snobbery indeed. Though, looking back, it did seem like a food revolution then. Vinegars were now varied and many, not just your mother's apple cider vinegar. Spaghetti was now pasta and to be cooked al dente, and vegetables were back to being fresh and steamed, or better yet, stir-fried, not out of the can or frozen and boiled to death. I was living in the middle of this revolution and my flag-waving, more often than not, was met with bemused stares and pushed-away food.

That's what I thought at the time. For all my Che Guevara-ness, all my let-me-show-you-what's-new-in civilized-cooking-ness, a simpler explanation was far more likely, I suspect when it came to crunchy, steamed broccoli—poor people have lousy teeth. They couldn't chew the broccoli, though nobody ever said that.

How do YOU cook fiddleheads? I asked my friend. We sauté them with a little oil and garlic. Ohh, I will try that, that sounds great.

What do they taste like? Someone asked me on the phone. I could visualize his nose scrunching up. Moss? Well, I laughed, I guess, maybe, a bit. It IS an acquired taste. We just grew up with them, in Maine and Massachusetts, so, if you're not used to them, I can maybe see them tasting like, well, the lawn.

I spread the heap out on a newspaper on the kitchen table. I found a paring knife and began to clean and trim them. No small task. I dug around for a pot, filled it with salted water and tossed the fiddleheads in at the boil. I boiled and boiled and boiled them.

I boiled them some more. I drained them. By now they resembled green mush. I had made the obligatory something else for dinner, but mainly ignored it. I put the fiddleheads on a plate, slathered on butter and scrounged the cabinet for the cider vinegar. There it is, in the back. By the layer of dust, it looked like nobody touched it since 2005. I sat at the table, plate of fiddleheads in front of me.

You and Rocky were down by the river all afternoon; did you get a lot of them?

Hey Dad, the New York Democrat is home, ha!

Turn off Fox News. I picked up some fiddleheads at Atkins, come help me clean them? Come on you, guys, it's balsamic vinegar, let's try that instead of cider. I don't know how they make it, but it's the thing, though lately.

IT TASTES WEIRD.

Shut up, Larry, it does not taste weird.

Hmmm.

I'm going to cook them al dente this time. That means cook a little less, so they retain some flavor and crunch. I think that means 'to the tooth.' I started watching cooking shows with Greg. Yes, Greg is good, he is always asking for you.

Now at the table, the silent table, I look at the plate in front of me. I think about packing some up to take to the nursing home. I pick up a fork.

Food LA

I don't eat... food, he said. He would always pause before he said food. Like, what? You don't eat... squirrels? You don't eat...monster trucks? Scott, what the fuck? What the fuck do you mean, you don't eat food? What the fuck does that mean? I don't eat food like the rest of you eat. Scott thought he was fat (we were fat, too). Scott was poor. We all were poor actors in Hollywood. Scott didn't drive. We often took my car to get around.

Scott, all those bitches are going to be over here tomorrow afternoon and we have to feed them something. This is your house, what do you want to feed them? He recently assumed the chairmanship of the play selection committee of our theatre company in Hollywood, and we were reading a new play the next day.

Let's liquor them up, he said. Oh, we'll do that, for sure, but we need SOME food. Get in the car, we'll get the heavy stuff you need, we'll get cat litter so you don't have to hump that.

Vegetables, dip, crackers, cheese, fruit. Somebody bought pastries. I made bloody marys in the kitchen. Our friends poured in the house the next day. The sun shone through the window, as the cats draped Scotty while he was seated, presiding over our world. After one of these gatherings I once asked him, apropos of our Hollywood career, is this it? He thought for a nano second and said yes, this is it. I fought Scott long and hard over that being that. This can't be it. We don't have Hollywood careers. We're doing plays at nonprofit theatres for zero money. We are at stupid day jobs. No, this may be it for you, bud, but it ain't it for me. I'll go back east. I'll go to New York and get a job in the real theatre, but this ain't it for me. Shall I make us some coffee? One of the kids left the pastries. I'll get us a pastry and some fruit and let's watch some dumb-ass movie. Or that Wahlberg porn thing, what was the name of that, where Phillip Seymour Hoffman makes an awkward pass at Marky Mark and then cries so hard about it that snot is rolling off his face. God, we love him. Let's do that. I'll get the joe brewing. Where's Tommy? He's supposed to be here soon. I'll fix a plate for him, now, too. Cause this ain't it, my Mary, no way, not by a long shot, this is not as good as it gets. Oh that's Tommy pulling up, let me scoot into the kitchen.

Yes, that was it, alright.

I should bring him something. I should bring him food. I should visit more often. I should do a lot of things. What is it that I'm not doing? What is it that I'm not doing I should feel so terrible about this? DID I just drop him off at the pound? AM I selling off his dog treats? HOW could I have forgotten to check the market last year for the fiddleheads? You didn't know it would be the last chance he might have to have one of his favorite foods. You didn't know that, did you? I thought about taking him some fiddleheads this year. I could cook them and take them to him in a Tupperware thing, butter, the cider vinegar, the whole thing. Why didn't I do that? I don't know why. There is a part of me trying to erase everything. All of it. I want it gone. I want this house gone. I want western Massachusetts to be gone. I want him gone. The struggle to come to grips with the past is too much, I want to be gone. So, I ignore. None of this is happening. Is this it? This can't be it. Is this it for him? Is this it for me? Is this it for him because he will never have another fiddlehead? What else is this for? Will he never have ice cream again? Pickles? Cucumbers in vinegar? Corn on the cob? He'll never have that oyster stew he makes, that I can't make as well. Tommy liked that in LA, but it wasn't as good.

Is this it, Scott? Was that it?

Food New York

What was the best meal you'd ever had? I could always answer that immediately. With Ruthie and Don on Cape Cod. Thirty years and I still remember that. Ruthie, her mother Endine, Don, Larissa, still a baby, Tom, Scott and myself. We were at Ruthie and Don's cottage on Wellfleet. Don went to the bay that afternoon for oysters. He came back and dumped a pail of oysters on the newspaper on the kitchen table. We cleaned, he shucked. Scott was squeamish, but the rest of us were happy to let a briny Wellfleet oyster slide down our throats that day. A briny Wellfleet oyster is the perfect bite. It wasn't even a bite, it was a glide. A glide down and then a slurp of the ocean from the shell. Scott would watch and shake his head.

Next, the lobster pot came out. As the water heated, a pile of lobsters was dumped on the table. At this point, Larissa was shuffled out of the kitchen, as she began to eye the live beings on the newspaper, then the boiling pot of water on the stove. We could see her start to put it together. Some of us formed an informal human wall around the pot, lest she come back. Behind the wall, our crustacean friends were quickly dispatched.

What makes the perfect meal? It's a combination of things. It's about the food, of course, but also who you're with, where you are.

On a screened-in porch in Wellfleet, thirty years ago, Ruthie's mother set down a green salad. I remember radicchio in the salad. I remember thinking, radicchio, those red leaves, ohh a fancy salad. I will have to try that back home. I wonder if they will eat that. Ruthie brought in a platter of corn on the cob. Scott, Tom and I sat around the long table and watched as the family bustled around us. Don wrangled the lobsters to the table. Larissa was collected and seated. She seemed not to put two and two and the eight-legged creatures together, and happily played with a claw. Everybody settled at the table in the Cape Cod gloaming and passed butter, salt and nutcrackers. Salad and corn took a spin around the table. Somebody showed Scott how to crack a lobster.

Yeah, Scott, this is it, too.

Food-NY-LA-Here

I got the call in LA. Can you come home for Thanksgiving? I remember thinking, what? I am never there, in Massachusetts, for Thanksgiving. Thanksgivings were elaborate affairs in New York, with much fussiness and fanfare. In LA, though, not as fussy, they were loud and long and crawling with actors and writers. I was in rehearsal for a play at that time, and wasn't planning on leaving Los Angeles, and I certainly wasn't going back to Massachusetts. Can you come home? She asked me on the phone, Can You Come Home? I hadn't talked to her in months, hadn't seen her for longer than that, not since the last time I came home and we had a massive blowout, because well, she is a psycho bitch. I never stayed in that house again. Can you come home and can you make the ambrosia and can you make cranberry sauce? Ambrosia? I had forgotten all about that. I think I made it a couple of times when I was in high school there. Cranberry sauce I had been making for years now, so, yes, I could make that, but ambrosia? Uhh, well, let me check in with Larry, I will stay with him, and let me see about flights. OK, let's go back there one last time. She had been sicker than usual, there was an ambulance at the house once every two weeks, it seemed. I vaguely listened as my brother or father would call me with the latest, but the truth is, I wasn't very interested. Call me when she's dead, I told them both, but they continued to call with updates. One last time, OK. But, ambrosia? She wants ambrosia.

I took time off from the play, but I had to return off-book, lines learned. Fine, two six-hour plane rides should get me off-book. Ambrosia?

In New York, pit stopping at my apartment with my roommate, I asked him, do you remember what ambrosia is? Shirley wants it for Thanksgiving. Oh yes, he says, all our (midwestern) mothers and grannies made that for a special occasion. Yes, Shirley says I used to make it in high school for Thanksgiving, ha, that must have been my attempt at foreign cuisine. There I was, making them try new things even at 16. You know what ambrosia is, Greg says, it's that foofey salad with marshmallows and those little oranges, and I think coconut. Oh, yes, I said, with maraschino cherries? And was it whipped cream or mayo base? What else was in it, something else? It did come back to me, not quite a dessert, not really a side. It was a tropical looking thing, it had bananas I think, as well, adding to the whimsy.

That night in New York I make cranberry sauce. A double batch; one for the crowd in New York, one for Massachusetts. Fresh cranberries, oranges, cloves, allspice, sugar and water. Stir until the cranberries just begin to pop. Chill. Best to chill for a few days, but overnight will do. The New York crowd, I suspect, doesn't really like fresh cranberry sauce (something about fruit and meat together) but they ooh and ahh just the same, to encourage me.

Thanksgiving morning my brother picks me up in Springfield and we ride to our parents' house.

Did you get the stuff for the ambrosia?

Yes, he said. I peer into the shopping bag.

No coconut. I say.

Oh, he says.

We stop for coconut.

How is she, I ask?

Not good, he says. She keeps going to the emergency room but they keep discharging her. She went last week, had some tests. I think they found something. A mass or something on her lungs.

Oh. I say. I wasn't interested enough to ask about follow ups, upcoming doctor appointments.

Oh. Yeah, when Dad called last week he said she wasn't good.

No, she's not, my brother said.

Uh huh. When is she going to die, I asked? The words hung in the frosty interior of my brother's Chevy. Like you could see them, as written on a steamed-up bathroom mirror, as written out as schoolboy piss in the snow, as a banner flown over a broiling August Coney Island beach.

When is she going to die?

Soon, I think, he says.

Larry and I walk in the ancient kitchen. They are sitting there at the rickety table. The kids have been prepping dinner. I smell turkey. I kiss my father, I approach her. Yes, she will die soon, I see; her eyes are frightened and wide. She thanks me for coming all your way. We don't hug, but say hello (somewhat fondly). For a second, I see a million sorrys flicker through her eyes. I send a million sorrys back in a blink, as we both know it's too late.

I turn to the kids, OK what's left to do? I brought the ambrosia stuff. Eyes light up, oh yes, make that now and we can put it in the fridge to chill. I fake my way through making it. Well, making is overstating it perhaps. I figure I just throw all this crap in a bowl. Hey, you kids got a bowl I can throw all this crap in? Marshmallows, cans of the mandarin oranges, coconut, sour cream, Cool Whip, pineapple and the maraschino cherries. Suddenly proud of my white trash heritage, I step back and gaze at the confection proudly. I show my mother the bowl and for an instant, we are transported back to a Thanksgiving before we were wrecked, before all was lost, before we were drunk and mean, before we escaped to New York and Los Angeles with our very life, and we were all just giddy about an exotic thing (is it a side? is it a dessert?) on the Thanksgiving table. Oh yes, she says! I remember that! She asks for a taste and we dig out spoons. We each take a spoonful and laugh, YUP that's it. OK, you two, it has to go into the refrigerator to chill. And leave some for the rest of us, one of the kids says.

OK OK, we say.

Hey, I made cranberries, too, I almost forgot. Mom's eyes light up at that, too. But hers were the only lit up eyes. My brother looks doubtfully at the jar of fresh cranberry sauce. Well, sis, he says, we have cranberries here, too. He gestures to the table where a can of cranberry jelly sits, ridged and wobbly. Larry, I say, that is in no way shape or form cranberry sauce. That is nasty from the can.

He laughs, that's how I like it, I like to see the lines the can makes

and it should be jiggly. Ughhh, I say, just try some homemade

sauce. He shakes his head. He has indoctrinated my nephew into

the anti-fresh camp. Stephen shakes his head. My mother giggles,

more for us.

Everything starts to hit at once and we crowd around the

rickety table. In the many years since I have been here for

Thanksgiving, the folks have turned to a ricer for the potatoes

instead of mashed. Out comes the turkey, Dad makes gravy over

two burners on the stove. The dressing is ladled out. The ambrosia

is fetched (the verdict being it was a side, not dessert). Larry has

taken over making the stuffing it seems. It used to be a mother

recipe-task, but she has handed that down to him. (On this last

Thanksgiving on earth, he, very sick from cancer, opted not to fly

home from North Carolina to be with his own family, but opted to

stay South, alone). He was very ill, and travelling would be hard,

but he did tell me the reason was so he could fix his own

Thanksgiving, the way he wanted it. That dressing, riced potatoes

and jiggly canned cranberries.

Everybody dug in. One old amusement: my mother always stood up to cut her meat and fix her potatoes, much to the amusement of everybody. Grandma, why do you stand up? I don't know, she would always screech back, I don't know, shut up and everybody laughed harder. This time, as she stood, and the decades-old question was lobbed over to her, I notice her nose dripping. Not the usual, oopsie, I have a cold and my nose is runny, but a pretty solid stream. Jesus, I thought, her spinal fluid is leaking.

She had taken me aside earlier in the day and shown me her discharge papers from the ER just a few days ago. She was discharged with pneumonia and a mass on her lung. I thought it odd the ER didn't keep her at least overnight, and there didn't seem to be any tests on the horizon. I asked her if she had a follow-up with her doctor. No, she said. (Oh, ER and doctors sending you home to die. Oh, I get it, yes.) She kept pointing to the phrase, mass on the lung, and looking at me, wild-eyed, afraid. I said, yes, ma I see that. I mumbled something about, better go see the doctor about that. Something useless and stupid like, better go see the doctor about that. And hey, let me grab the butter from the refrigerator cause dinner is almost on the table.

And now, there she was, standing over potatoes, cutting her turkey, spinal fluid dripping a solid stream. She starts to cry, I don't want to die, she wails, I don't want to die. Silence fell over the table. The kids looked down. Larry reached for a cigarette. I sighed inwardly and wondered when my flight back to LA was the next morning, was it 7:30 or 8:30? Was I all packed? A few more things to cram into the suitcase, I think. Oh, yes, better find that script, you have to learn your lines on the plane, God, I have a couple of tricky monologues, that's going to be tough on the plane, I better check that itinerary, damn, it's in my purse in the living room I would have to scramble over 4 people to get it, fuck it, just live through this moment.

I don't want to die, she keened again. My father was the courageous one here.

You're not going to die, he said. Once or twice he said that. You're not going to die.

After awhile, she settled down. She sat down. We ate in relative silence. The turkey is good. The ambrosia is good. The potatoes are good. People said things were good intermittently. Uh huh, yeah, this is good.

The kids and I did the dishes and tin-foiled everything and then Larry and I collected ourselves to leave. She was still sitting at her place at the table. I bent down to kiss her cheek. Her frightened eyes looked up at me. Goodbye Ma.

In the car, Larry and I unraveled. Jesus Christ. WHEN is she going to die, one of us says. Soon, I think, the other one says.

Two days later my father tells me on the phone I think that will be the last time you see her as if I didn't know that.

Food Here and Now

Seven years later, my mother and brother dead, my father in late stages Alzheimer's, on the Monday morning before Christmas, I watch Debbie mop down the lacquered hallway towards me. The College was quiet; I was first in.

How was the party? Oh, it was fun. Everybody brought something. I made these little meatballs and brought them in a crock pot. I have this recipe where you use grape jelly. Really?? I say, grape jelly? I've never heard of that. Yes, she says, you throw it in with a bunch of chili sauce. They were good. OH, I love chili sauce, I'll try that. Yes, she says, it was fun to all get together and eat and hang out.

We didn't get a raise this year, though. Oh. I'm sorry. Oh, well. Debbie pushed the mop around under the conference table. I'm sorry, I said again. That doesn't seem fair. No, she said. The early morning winter sun twinkled through the windows, reflecting off the shiny floor.

Oh, the Spanish girl made the rice. It was good. This year everybody loved it. I bet! I say. The smoked pork and the olives and all those spices! Yes, she says, it was so good. I'd like to figure out how to make that, she says. Me too! I say, I'd love to make that. Maybe I'll ask her for the recipe, Debbie says. Oh, do ask her. I bet that's a great dish to sit around and have with a bunch of people. Yes, ask the Spanish girl for the recipe. I'd love to have it too. Debbie nods and I watch her mop her way back down the hallway.

The Easy Table

Look at me look at me look at me look at me don't look at me.

I got to the meeting before he did. I sat alone at one of the rounds and busied myself with the purse contents, hauling out a pen, capping and uncapping it. I rummaged for a notebook, scrounged for the phone, all the while furtively looking at the door. No, not yet. The hall started to fill up, nobody I was particularly close to was there. Great, now I'll be sitting alone or alone with co-workers I barely know. I panic a bit. It really is too much to think he'll sit with you.

We had an odd, uncomfortably awkward encounter the last time he was in my office. I had carefully planned what pointless memo I was going to make unnecessary photocopies of as he came into the office. I breezed a breathy oh, hi there, all surprised, as I blew past him to the copy room. I skulked by the copier as I heard the rest of his group assemble in the outer area. As the group began to move collectively past the copy room on the way to the inner office, and he was safely past me, I ventured to the door and heartily and too-loudly wished a colleague of his a vastly warmer greeting. Hi, how have you been? Great to see you. I wondered at the time why I did that. I picked up the uncopied memo and went back to my desk.

I started to think about the urgent phone calls I will have to make as the end of the meeting approached. I heard the inner office door open and the murmur of the group as it approached. I snapped around and grabbed the phone, dialing furiously my father's ancient number, now ringing into the blackness, never to be answered.

I could feel him behind me, waiting. I pretended I couldn't feel him. I put the phone down, irritated that my Very Important Phone Call wasn't being answered. I waited a beat, (I can still feel him behind me, waiting) sniffed, and decided to call my Very Important Phone Call's assistant. I busily call the ancient number again, ring ring into the blackness and somewhere in there I hope my daddy will answer. No. No answer.

I have been out-waited. I put the phone down and swivel to him.

Hi, he says. Hi, I say. Everything's good? I ask. Everything's good, he says. Silence, as both of us bubble up with the unspoken. It's good to see you, he says. Yes, it's good to see you, I say. He partially turns around (the rest of the group has moved away). He turns back and comes to me. He bends down and hugs me. It's good to see you, both of us blather again.

I won't see you I won't see you looking at me you won't see me looking at you.

The hall is really beginning to fill up now. People I vaguely know sit beside me. I move my purse from the chair next to me. (For real, are you saving him a seat, for real?) The featured speaker enters and fusses with AV, an easel, whatever else speakers need. People start milling about the breakfast buffet directly behind me. A colleague sits next to me and talks. We talk for a few minutes. I keep up appearances, I chitty chat about whatever she is talking about, grateful to hold my own.

He comes through the door and talks to all in his wake. He is a well-spoken, popular guy. He doesn't see me (I think) and takes the easy table, far from me. Ahh, yes, the easy table. His immediate work crew, people from various departments I know that he is safe with. He doesn't look around the room but I know he knows where I am.

I choke and turn away from my chatty colleague, fussing in my purse for a Kleenex to clean my glasses. She doesn't notice anything, thank God. What a long four hours this will be.

I scoot my chair so that he is blocked, I can't see him.

Canyouseemecanyouseemecanyouseeme?

I see him rise and head toward the back, towards the breakfast buffet, towards me. Wow, what a great time for an urgent phone call, I think. I turn my chair slightly and I pull my hair down on my left side so when he passes he won't see my face, I think.

Lookatmelookatmelookatmelookatmedon'tlookatme.

He stops behind my chair, talking to all who linger there. I dial the ancient number hurriedly, importantly. My father doesn't answer in the blackness so I dial the Very Important Phone Call's assistant, again.

He doesn't wait for me this time. He moves to the buffet. I hang up on the assistant, the black abyss.

He returns to the easy table. I adjust my seat and hair so I can't see him, he can't see me. For four hours I adjust, I move slightly, scraping my chair this way and that. I toss my hair side to side so YOU CAN'T SEE ME AND I CAN'T SEE YOU.

Don't look at me don't look at me don't look at me look at me why aren't you looking at me I look at you all the time I know you like to look at me I know you like to talk to me I know this would have been the ideal thing for us to have done together I know you can't I am sick of men who want to and can't.

The thing ends. I talk to my table, my chatty colleague. Oh yes, how valuable, what a lesson learned, how instructive, we say. He is turned around, back to me, full on with the easy table. I rustle up my bags, my notebooks, my Kleenex and wonder what the recovery period will be on this one. I say my goodbyes to my tablemates, as I take mental odds of the probability of throwing up before I reach the door.

I ready myself and break for the exit, swish past the easy table, head thrown back, laughing gaily with the phone pressed against my ear as the Very Important Phone Call's assistant answers, finally. I reach the car and throw everything in the backseat. I sit at the wheel for a while. I see people start to exit the building and that rousts me to kick in gear, start the car and drive. I don't want to get caught hi, hi, hi-ing anyone here, much less…

Drive anywhere. I stop for gas and can't figure out why the nozzle doesn't fit my gas tank. I wrestle with that for a while. It's a new car, I think (well, new for me, it's actually pretty old). Maybe that's it, I think. This new old car, maybe it's so old the gas tank is made differently so the gas nozzles don't fit any more. That's my luck, the car guys should have told me I would have trouble gassing the car with this old-timey gas tank that nozzles don't fit into any more. That's hardly fair. They should have told me. I try again. No, the nozzle doesn't fit. I feel a wave of nausea wash over me and I rock back against the new old car. Leaning against her, panting, I look around and see I am at the diesel pump. Oh. That's probably it. Pushing off the car, I lurch to the regular gas pump. Yeah, this fits. That must have been it.

I drive back to the office. It's getting dark earlier. Lights are coming on. It smells like fall, it smells like purple gloaming. The nearby market has red and gold stuff all around, what? Vegetables? Yes, it must be red and gold vegetables they are putting out now. As I drove by I didn't notice the specific vegetables but I did notice as red and gold and purple rushed through me; I noticed as fall blew through me.

I step into the office. She isn't nice to me. She sometimes can be nice and she isn't as bad as she was at being nice to me, but she isn't nice to me now. Didn't anyone notice I wasn't there? she barked. She's like that. It has to be about her. Even though she is thirty years younger than my mother when she died, she's like my self-involved mother. I cringe. Yes, I asked Belinda where you were, and she said you were skipping this, you didn't feel like it, you had stuff to do. That mollified her. As long as she was given her due, was asked about. She leaves shortly thereafter. Good. I sit in the darkened office. Rain hits the window and I watch the purple gold red fade into blue black. I smell coffee though there is no coffee on.

After school, I would walk down the hill, by the ballfield. It was a long hill and I would walk slowly. In the fall, there would be ballgames. I stopped sometimes to watch them play. Then on I would trudge. When I turned the corner, I could see the house around another bend. It was a good sign if the truck was parked there. Dad was home so maybe it wouldn't be so brutal. I would open the door and sometimes there would be coffee on. It was a tremendous relief to smell the coffee on. On those nights we were almost normal, she was almost normal. Dad would cook something. She was capable of sitting at the table with us and we had an almost normal dinner. We would play with the dog and maybe watch TV or play a game after dinner. Maybe we're almost normal, I would think. When I would turn that corner, past the ballpark, and see the truck in the yard and see a light on in the kitchen, twinkling in the red gold purple autumn and I could smell the coffee from up the hill, I was so happy thinking we might be almost normal tonight, my brother and I wouldn't be alone and frightened in the chaos, but almost normal, drinking coffee and playing with the dog.

I got to be normal in New York. I would work late downtown. Greg and I lived uptown. I would close up the office, say goodbye to the neighbors next door and hustle out into the New York twilight. The lights were just coming on as nine million of us headed home. Fall nipped at my heels as I headed for the 6 train. I knew Greg would have started dinner. I wonder what tonight, a chicken leg? Bum what's for dinner? A chick leg with lima beans and a rolled tate. Mmmm. Can't wait! Or, during an election year it would be Primary Pot Pie. The best was if Greg and I were going to a show that evening, I would say, when asked during the day, Oh Greg and I are going out tonight, we're seeing that thing that opened last week. Yes, that was the best. I belonged. I was someone's family. We were each other's family and we were normal and we did things together, cooked for each other, went to plays together, had our friends over. We had two cats.

I sat in the office awhile more and watched the purple gold turn into charcoal outside the window. The New York lights and the smell of coffee down the hill swirled around inside me.

Ohhhh, you're un-familied. That's what it is. You're un-familied. Your father is lying in a nursing home, the coffee won't be on when you come down the hill. Greg won't have that chick leg in the oven and you won't be going to that thing that opened last week. Anyway, there is no one to tell about going to that thing that opened last week, rather defeating the purpose of going to that thing. Belinda would have been fun to tell about that, she would have laughed and asked about it. Belinda and I should go to a thing, I think.

I hoist up and shut off the lights in the office. I haul my un-familied self to the car.

Driving, it occurs to me I need to cut the Easy Table some slack. None of this is his fault. I open the window. Oh hey, this new old car has power windows. Ha, I have never had a car with power windows. I play with the windows a bit, breathing in the night air. The windows are fun. I pull into the driveway of the old, dark shack. I open the door to the two circling meowing cats.

I snap on all the lights and put a pot of coffee on.

Is It the Dog's Birthday?

How many essays do you have? the writing teacher asked.

Oh, I don't know, maybe 12.

Really, you seem to be cranking them out? Hmm, maybe you should do a table of contents.

Yeah, I guess.

I had been meaning to do a table of contents, but how boring right? I suspect I haven't been wanting to look at the whole thing. The big picture, ugh. Somehow that shit would get realer if I looked at it that way. Somewhere in this retreat we had been talking about the mechanics of a book. How many pages, how many words? I forget the pages, but somewhere in there 78,000 stuck.

God I'm tired. I should get up at some point. Memorial Day Weekend. Three days of unstructured time. I used to look forward to that. Now it doesn't matter if I am working or not working. If I'm working at least I have to shower and think about some semblance of color coordinating a fetching outfit. Why does that cat box stink like a motherfucker? That new litter blows. It was lightweight, that new light kind. That's why you bought it. You were at the Big Y, just out from visiting the nursing home.

I forced myself to shop that day.

It's hot, I can barely push the cart. I should call the physical therapist, any physical therapist. It's not helping you are still reeling from that car accident. Well, reeling is perhaps overstating it, but it's painful, even more painful than usual to stand for five minutes. OK, so we are running out of gas just pushing the shopping cart. The litter is on the other end of the store. Fuck. Stand in the deli line for crab cakes? No, I don't care anymore, grab fish sticks on the way past frozen foods. Do I REALLY have to go all the way to the other end of this goddamn store? What do I have at home? I have a big jug of Pinot in the fridge. Yeah, fish sticks and Pinot. That's all I can manage anyway. I can cancel the rest of this and just barely make it to the checkout line, I am starting to sweat and shake. It's all been a bit much for one day, no? Dad didn't look so good today, that weird thing is growing on his back. I'm going to have to talk to a doctor about that. God it's hot in here. I could use a nap. I wonder if I curled up next to the kidney beans anybody would notice. Maybe I don't have to go all the way to the cat litter aisle, maybe not. FUCK, they're out of food, too. That's right. I can slide on the litter another day or so, but somehow those two furry freaks are insistent upon eating. Alright, we can do it. If I position most of my upper body over the cart, I can roll myself to the other end, push off with one foot. Roll me away. I roll up the pet aisle, panting like a sheepdog locked inside a Toyota in July. I realize I am more fucked than a bagful of kittens headed to the lake.

I bet you have more than you think, he says. You've been churning them out since last time. Let's just see what you got. Let's see where you're at.

I think about this. I don't think I have. But maybe I have. I retreat, envious of my colleagues who have slightly more fun assignments. I start counting essays and assemble them in somewhat chronological order, though I know that may change later.

Rolling past toilet paper (fuck do I need toilet paper, fuck it I don't care, I have paper towels still, I think) I hit the pet aisle. Grab a few cans of Friskies wet–pate, not shredded, and eye cat litter. I might as well, I'm here. I am really feeling ill in the heat, though. You can't carry this heavy stuff, no way. Though the load is lightened with all the things you didn't buy as you bargained your way out of this shopping trip. Good call on the fish sticks, way lighter than crab cakes. I know I won't be able to hoist the heavy litter into the cart. Then I spy it. 50% lighter! Lightweight biodegradable container! A variety of fragrances: Cherry Apple Orchard, Lilac Rose Garden, Vanilla Cinnamon Buddha Pie. 50% Lighter! As I feel myself slipping down the cart, I grab the lightweight litter and toss it (almost effortlessly) in the cart. Weeping with relief, I head to the checkout. The lady looks at me kindly as I hang on to the little electronic payer-thing, swiping the first card I could grab. Sweating, swallowing down bile, I make idle chit chat, as human beings do. (Please don't notice that I am collapsing, please don't notice my weird breathing, please don't

notice that I am alone here in this part of the country I never wanted

to be back in for a second taking care of someone who never had a

chance in hell himself, who never made a sacrifice for me yet I am

sacrificing everything, my friends, my art, my way of life, please

don't notice any of this.) Pretty hot, today, huh? I chirp, as I

(artfully, or so it seems to me) switch my death-clutch from the

electronic payer-thing back to the cart as to avoid fainting outright.

Wow, I should make those two little furry boys get jobs, huh? as the

pate and NEW! Lightweight Apple Orchard roll through, maybe

totaling twelve bucks. The cashier looks at me, laughs nervously

and looks around. Oh yes, she says. Someone has joined her, as if an

invisible Cashier Bat Signal has gone up. The second cashier starts

to bag, eyes me, says cheerily, Wow, sure is hot. Eyes me again.

Will you need help out to your car, ma'am?

I roll back over. Jesus Christ it's hot. The cat litter stench is

almost suffocating. Didn't I change that box yesterday, the day

before? I don't really remember. Maybe I will change it today.

What day is it? Saturday? Oh yes, Saturday, Sunday, Monday.

Great three days. I have three days to change the litter. Drag a mop over these floors, go see Pops in the Shady Rest, try to shop again, pick a lucky winner from the frightening pile of bills. No, you don't even have to pick a winner, maybe just arrange by category and then peek at the bank accounts, settle for that. Deal with that pile of laundry, sitting there for the past week like Kilimanjaro. You have to write, you have to exercise, you have to figure out doctor appointments.

I roll back over and fall asleep.

Back in the hotel room, I am counting and arranging essays. Some are shorter, do I count those? Yes, I decide because I can come back and fill those out later. The later works are the longer ones, the ones I am growing into, the ones where I say what I really mean to say. I re-read a couple, yes that's the right track. This is how I want to bear witness. Maybe I DO have something here. I stack, I re-arrange. By time-line? By traumatic incident? By cities where I live? I decide on timeline. I keep stacking.

Next day, one-to-one time, he asks me? How many do you have, Betty? Twenty-six, I say. I say again, twenty-six. Twenty-

161

six, he says? WOW. I know, right? Right? Oh my God. Yes, he says, I knew it. You have been cranking them out. Have I? I ask. Yes, he says. The word count is 35,000. 35,000. I seem to remember 78,000 is a book. That's probably not right, but I don't care. I have half a book done. I am halfway through my book.

I wake up. Noon. Christ. Get up, you have to get up. What time is it again? Oh yeah, noon. God I'm tired. The cats yowl. What day is it? Saturday. What do I have to do today? Jesus H, bills, Kilimanjaro, Pops in the home, mop-dragging, write, exercise. Also, don't forget to be a normal person. See friends. Well, OK, you don't have to actually SEE them. Talk via text, IM, maybe that will be enough. Pretend it's fine, they won't know.

I put coffee on. I stumble back to the couch. Why the hell does that litter stink so much? It's the new litter I bought this week, that's what it is. NEW! 50% lighter! Apple Orchard Fresh. It smells like a cat shit in the orchard. Yeah, I got to change that box today, add that to the list, I'll do that. What time is it, noon? I flick on the TV. Damn, I missed all the Saturday Good Eats episodes. Now I am stuck with that stupid pioneer woman with her redneck-husband-on-the-ranch-bullshit. I hate-watch that for a while. What time is it now? Close enough to whatever time I need it to be. I pour some wine. Hey, it's the weekend, I have three days ahead to do all that stuff. I heat something up in the microwave. I pour some more wine.

I think about going to see Dad. No, there's two more days for that. I slip in a Tony Shalhoub Monk DVD. I watch two episodes. I eat something else. I cry over the one where Mr. Monk has to give back the kid he is fostering 'cause Mr. Monk can't take care of him. It's so unfair that Mr. Monk can't have that kid, why can't he have that little piece of happiness? But, no, Mr. Monk can't take care of the kid, I know it's the right thing to do, I know in my heart of hearts Mr. Monk can't take care of that kid. The new family the kid gets looks alright, I guess. I cry some more anyway. I watch two more. Two easier ones, ones where Randy fucks something up or something. Easy. I walk past the cat box, closing my eyes and holding my breath. Yes, I will do that today, yes, I will. I veer past Kilimanjaro. Well, I should do that today as tomorrow or the next day there will be more laundry to replace that pile. I stop briefly by

163

the pile, decide against doing anything about it and think about walking back to the couch.

I think about my father. Maybe I will see him tomorrow. Maybe I won't. My leg really hurts from that car accident a few weeks back. I stretch halfheartedly. It really hurts to walk down that long hallway to the lockdown ward where dad is now. I must stop halfway and rest on a chair before resuming the long journey to the end of the hall, ring the buzzer for entre to the loony bin. Too long of a walk, I think to myself. I can't deal with that today. And anyway, fuck him, why should I? Why should I be here for any of this? And now I have to drag my limpy leg down that fucking long hall where I have to pit stop halfway fucking down. I always pretend I am stopping on one of the halfway chairs to take a VERY important phone call so the nurses and aides don't mistake me for a wayward resident or a decrepit visiting family member. Yeah, fuck him, I don't want to go today. Maybe I will go tomorrow.

I think about writing. Why aren't I writing? It's been about six months since we did that table of contents thing and I wrote something in addition up there in Woodstock. I haven't written since. I blame work. Too much time at a job for less money than it takes to float this hellhole in the first place. (Thanks for leaving me this falling down motherfucker, pops, one more thing to thank you for.)

Too many things happened at the same time: the Alzheimer's finally becoming too terrifying to be safe, this opportunity to change over to work at the college where I want to be, the house flipped over into my name, oops, only a year contract at the college, that's OK, sign, sign, sign, it will take you a year to unload this hellhole anyway. Maybe I shouldn't have signed; a year more will kill you here. It's killing you already. Yeah, really, fuck him, I'll go tomorrow. I'm too tired today. Why am I so tired today? What time is it now?

I think all these things as I lurch back to the couch. I think all these things at the same time, I am aware that my brain is in overdrive on this very short walk. All these thoughts flash through like whizzing lightning bolts. My head must be on fire, right? I am tempted to stick my head out the window and holler to the neighbors, hey, guys, notice anything? Anything particularly, well, ablaze, above my shoulders? You'd tell me, right? No, nothing? OK, thanks.

I land back on the couch. Can I do another Monk? One more to calm me, one more to put out the fire.

I do that. I choke on cat litter fumes. I drink more wine. I don't write. I feed the cats their dinner though I don't think it's their dinner time.

I think I need to go to bed.

I go to bed. You're in some trouble here, sister. You're in some pretty bad trouble. What are we doing about this trouble? I wonder if it is ordinary, usual, trouble or trouble trouble. I think maybe trouble trouble as I fall asleep. I sleep for the rest of the day, the rest of the night.

Hey, it's Sunday, we should do something? Do you want to go for a drive? Let's head east, over towards Worcester, we can drive by that pretty lake? I know you like to be by the water, we will stop at that café we drove by last month. What a pretty drive that will be. Now, stop all that writing and come on, I get a chance to have you, too, you know. The next book isn't due until March, that draft isn't due until October, you can give me one afternoon by the water, can't you?

I throw my head back and laugh gaily. OH YOUUU, I say. Alright, just this one, then tomorrow I really have to get back at it. But yes, today is yours.

I dress in a white roadster outfit (I don't even know what a white roadster outfit is, but for the purposes of this sequence, I want it to be that). I toss a gauzy white scarf around my scarlet locks and off we go.

How beautiful you are today, he says. I look at him and lower my eyes modestly. He is also dressed in a roadster outfit (God knows, I don't know). He has always been kind and lovely to me. We talk, we laugh, the wind is through our hair.

The café is on the lake. It is a little before noon, so it hasn't filled up yet. I can tell the hostess recognizes me, a secret smile as she leads us to a table by the window. He pulls my chair out.

I haul out of the pickup, stumble to the nearest table and fall into a chair. I toss my purse to the empty side of the table, yammer something about a Bloody Mary to the perky blonde waitperson.

I look over the lake. It is somewhat overcast. There is a deck outside and one lower, to the right. The servers are huddled in

167

a gaggle around the end of the bar, gearing up for the shift. They are not talking about me.

Oh yes, it is good to get away for a time, aren't you clever by half? You are so right, I did need a break from publishers, deadlines and all that. (I also think 'a break from line-learning, directors, opening night jitters' and realize I am mixing up artistic areas, but I don't care, as I'm sure, I have to give him a name today, I'll call him Jay, Jay doesn't care. Though it is a sign that this particular dream ballet is wearing thin. No matter, take it as far as it will go.)

When are you going into the City, he asks? Well, I guess I should scoot in next week, what do you think? I do need to get in to see Sid (the agent) and he and the team need to look at these last two chapters before they send it to the publisher.

Jesus Christ it's hot in here. Where is that Bloody Mary? Well, at least I'm by the water. I haven't seen a soul in two days. God this weekend is endless. One more day of this? I'd rather be working.

I think about what happened in Los Angeles a couple of months ago. We haven't spoken, emailed or texted since. I suppose I have fucked that up, too. Don't think about that, not now, for

God's sake why are you thinking about that now? Don't, don't think of that. Look at the lake. Look at the lake. I look at the lake.

Hahaha, darling, look at that charming little paddleboat, over there. How do those ladies hold on, dressed in those long white day dresses and clutching those parasols? I laugh gaily (again) and toss back my scarlet locks (again).

I should have washed my hair. When was the last time I washed my hair? I rummage for a scrunchie. This purse is too big, loose change, gas receipts, broken makeup compacts that it is far too late for. I find a scrunchie balled up and attempt to wad some hair through it.

The Bloody Mary arrives. The blond waitperson cheerily asks me if I'm ready. Am I ready?

I blubber up something like fish and chips and off she goes.

I look back at the lake. I see a duck family, mama and paddling babies. There is a speedboat hauling a jet-skier. That looks like fun. I wish I could swim.

The lake reminds me of the camp. Dad would like it here. Though he would say it is fancy, for the sports. Will I ever bring him out of the home, to a place on a lake again, for lunch? Probably not. It's too much work, I'm selfish, I'm not doing enough, I'm not trying hard enough. Before the first Bloody Mary sip, I start to cry.

Why don't I come into the City with you, he says? After you meet with Sid, we can see a show, or that new ballet? Ohh darling, I say, no need really, I am just in and out. I'll be back Thursday. He looks crestfallen, there in his roadster whites. Really, I will be so busy with these meetings, and I do hate dragging you along for them, you'll be so bored. He looks down, pushing his radicchio around the plate.

Blah Blah, you're not trying hard enough, you're selfish, yeah yeah, you're in a public place, pull yourself together. I stop crying for a minute. I discreetly (I think) wipe my face. I look back at the lake. More people are out in boats. Kids are running on the banks. The café is filling up. The fish and chips arrive and I am presentable enough to look away from the window, nod directly to whom, whom? Amy is her name. Thank you, Amy, no nothing else, thank you. Her bright smile dims a bit and she glances back at me as she slips away.

Fuck. Now it's a thing, now I'm sitting here crying and it's a thing for the staff. Fuck. I turn back to the window, to the Georges

Seurat world beyond the glass. I push away all the I'm-a-Terrible-Daughter-Can't-Even-Take-Your-Father-Out-To-a-Nice-Lunch-by-a-Lake-That-You-Know-He-Would-Like terrors.

I push that away and I think about the thing that happened in Los Angeles. I cry even harder.

A *forkful of frisee halfway lifted, he says, I don't understand why you won't let me in that part of your life. Why can't I see your New York friends, go along to the agent's office? I could be helpful, you know, in negotiations. His blond hair, his gleaming teeth, his puppy dog eyes, truth be told, were getting tiresome. He's not usually the type I go for, what was I thinking? Darling, I am perfectly capable of negotiating, you know that, silly. I think I'm going to the opera, you don't like the opera. I see him getting upset, the corners of his mouth start to tremble. Oh darling, really, don't be that way. I'll be back in a few days, I need a little space to handle my business affairs and to see friends. In fact, I need a little more space in general. Can't you see that...*

Wait a minute, wait a minute, am I fighting with my imaginary boyfriend? I am breaking up, in a bit of a scene...with my imaginary boyfriend?

I pull my tear-stained face off the glass separating me from The Sunday in the Park world. I pull back errant strands of dirty hair fallen from the scrunchie. I look down at the fish and chips. I cry harder. The gaggle of staff near the bar collectively look at me, collectively slightly turn away. Amy breaks off and glides kindly over. She slips me napkins and I mop down my face. I calm myself enough to look around, thinking I am presentable. A biker slips into a nearby table. He doesn't notice me. I am calm enough to eat a couple of bites. No, I'm not calm enough after all. I turn back to the window, the lake. I should call and fix that fucked-up thing in LA with him. That thing was my fault. You're not to blame.

There is a family outside, in Seurat world, at one of the picnic tables. Kids, a dog, a goofy, shaggy dog. They are taking pictures and they corral the dog in the center of the shot. I wonder if it's the dog's birthday.

I wipe my face again. I can get down half the fish. You're not presentable and you need to leave. You are a mess and you shouldn't be in public. You need to get a grip, you really do. Leave the food, leave the drink. I signal for the check. It quickly appears. I hand over a card, no, you can just take it, I don't need to see the

172

total. I get up to leave, the gaggle looks away. I think I hear them sigh in relief. The biker has a draft beer and is looking out the window. At the door, I look back. I see him in a fleeting instant: his head in his hands, sunglasses off, white roadster jacket over his chair. I turn away.

I hoist myself up into the pickup (not the smart MG). Still crying, but not as badly, I back out. No scarf on my scarlet locks, my scrunchie falls out. At a light, I tie back my hair. I look over to the empty passenger seat. I drive the pickup back to the house, alone.

Inside, I change the cat litter. No, that New! Fresh Apple Orchard is out. Back to Tidy Cats or whatever. I make a grocery list (more Tidy Cats). I make a list of doctors I need to call. You need to call and see all these doctors because you are in some kind of trouble, missy. That's the plan for next week. Yes.

It's midday, but I fall asleep for a long time.

Monday, Memorial Day. I stop at the supermarket to pick up some things. VA Ray was outside, handing out the red poppies. He hands me a couple. No. No need to make a donation, he says. Thank your father for his service.

I drive the backroads to the Shady Rest, past Atkins, the large farmer's market. We used to come here when it was just an apple stand. In later years, on rare occasions when I could stand to be back within three thousand miles of this area, we would escape her and come to Atkins. A cider doughnut, some coffee, we would sit by the window and look at the Notch, that odd, jagged mountain that watched over us. We would just sit, quietly. Sometimes we would talk about her and the terror that tore through our family then, years without end. More often not, though.

I drove past the college that I loved, where I worked, where I now had friends, where I now had sanctuary.

I pull into the Shady Rest and navigate the long hallway. I pull out my phone on the Halfway Chair, though I don't worry so much about being taken for a patient or a feeble relative. (Well, you ARE a feeble relative, Betty). I look around. I study the daily menu posted right above me. Mmmmmm, oven baked chicken. Nurses, aides walk by, say hi to me. A volunteer with a little dog comes by. I play with the dog a bit. I get up and limpy-limp down the rest of the hallway. At the end, I ring the buzzer to the lockdown ward and enter. I pass the usual howling, wandering souls who sit, shake, lurk in the hallway and turn into my father's room. He is asleep, as usual. He is asleep 80 percent of the time now. Good for him, as it should be. I sit by the bed, nudge him a bit. Hi Dad. Hi babe, he says. He calls everybody babe, to the immense amusement of the ward. I'm sorry I haven't been in a while, I haven't been feeling very well, I say. Are you sick? he asks, alarmed. Oh, nothing serious, Dad. Don't worry, I'm going to the doctor and I'll be fixed up soon, not to worry. Hey, I ran into Ray at Stop and Shop. You remember Ray, from the VA? He came to the house a few months ago and helped us with the VA benefits? I know he doesn't remember but he says he does. Well, Ray asked me to give you a poppy, it's Memorial Day. Ray says thank you for your service. Oh, that's nice. We sit for a few more minutes, not talking. OK, Dad, get some sleep. I turn on the TV for him and leave.

When I get back to the house, I start calling doctors.

I'm Seeing a Bunch of Bitches Later

I'm seeing a bunch of bitches later, I blithely tell Lana, my bartender. I toss it out, seemingly almost bored, as if it is too much trouble to see this bunch of bitches later. God, those bitches are intrusive. They always want to get together; they are clingy, needy; clamoring for attention. They are always borderline hysterical when I simply don't have the time for them.

What are you going to do tonight (with the bitches)? Are you going out?

Ewww, a tough one. I didn't anticipate a specific question about the bitches, like, are they real? Like, who are they, what are you doing with them, where are you going with them? Think fast.

No, we're just hanging out at someone's house.

OK, so, the scenario now is perhaps one of the bitches is working late, that's why I am in this bar now, having dinner. (Wouldn't the bitches have dinner going?) Yeah, that's a hole in this set-up, maybe Lana won't notice that it is odd that the bitches are dinner-less, today of all days. Just talk faster and maybe Lana won't ask any more questions. If she does, however, now the movie is, yeah, one bitch working late, the rest of the bitches are hanging the crepe paper and loading the cupcakes and punch into somebody's basement. Spit that out if she asks again. Though wait a minute, that cupcake, streamers-in-the-basement thing was somebody's Sweet 16 (not even yours). So, now, if asked, you're panicking and mixing up parties real and imagined, not usually yours, of different decades. Don't panic, she won't ask. You won't have to trot out the late-working bitch and cupcakes.

There are no bitches waiting. Zero bitches are hanging streamers and baking cupcakes.

The isolation has been the worst of it.

My father has been unable to initiate or contribute much to conversation lately. I can see the disease carve away parts of him.

There never was much conversation anyway, though, frankly. Upon my departure, nobody was particularly interested in whatever I had going on in New York or Los Angeles. On my few return trips back over the years, I, too, was profoundly uninterested in their small-town life. We had successfully remained uninterested in each other up until now.

Until now.

Though we're together, I am alone.

I chat with the cat. We discuss the pros and cons of being a cat: free and loose, dodging traffic, losing fights to the neighbor cats, freezing in the sub-zero February nights. I talk to the pharmacists about thirty day supplies and dosings and why we are running through that particular med. I talk to the nice meals-on-wheels lady, Yes, Dad is OK, as well as can be expected, thanks, sure come in and say hello he loves to see you, oops, watch the open door, the goddamned cat will make a break for it.

I talk to the cashier, No, thanks, I'm not collecting stamps for the glasses.

I talk to the ladies at the local pub, I'm good, doll, how are you? Busy tonight, yes, he's fine, thanks for asking. These women are my favorites (except for Lila, my one real friend here). They are the friend substitutes. They are pretend friends. They know my food, drink. While we don't really talk talk; I listen as they talk to others, nod and sit among their friends as they talk talk. Close enough. It'll have to do.

Conversations with New York, Los Angeles, Chicago (other, past lives, busy lives, gone now? Really gone?) mainly through text, Facebook. One person calls, every other day-ish. It is hard to talk on the phone these days; it takes energy. I have to muster up the strength to answer the phone. Phone calls make me sleepy. It is far easier to text, IM. Short bursts of information are what I can handle.

The rule is: No spending the night under this roof on birthdays, award show days, New Year's Eve. There were always people around on any of those occasions. We gathered at restaurants, homes, fancy hotels. We cooked, we catered, we drove hours, took endless subways to be together. To spend any one of those days here, under this falling-down roof, in this shack that smells vaguely of piss and puke, shooing the cat from the door, changing the diapers on an uncomprehending old man (why can't he understand about the diaper changing) is unthinkable.

Dad we do this twice a day every day. He looks at me blankly, seated on the toilet. What do you want me to do? I am strapping on the gloves. I look at him. Dad same exact deal twice a day do you not understand we have to change your underthings so you don't get sick do you not remember we do this in the morning and at night? Well, no I don't see the necessity. He doesn't see the necessity he tells me. Well, I am telling you we need to do this twice a day. (What the FUCK is with him not remembering that, every fucking day the same argument. It is an odd thing for him not to remember, what the FUCK is with that, is it just an old person thing, is it a dementia thing? When the FUCK is his next doctor appointment again I have to ask about that, add that to the list of things I need to ask because this scene playing out twice a fucking day is working my last nerve.)

So far this year, so good. New Year's away, Johnny in Red Bank. Asbury, Roger, Rachel. Fine. Then New York for a few days. Good.

Now, though, a bad double-whammy weekend has dawned. A town committee obligation is keeping me here as two of the Rule days are occurring within three days of each other. I had thought of booking into a motel for those two days. That is what I usually do. That way, I am away. I am in a pretend place. Maybe meeting a lovah, maybe touring a play, maybe a hotel after a film shoot. I pretend I am in a long, flowy thing, bathrobe, dressing gown (usually doesn't matter which). There I can actually talk to friends on the phone as I am not so tired. I talk to real friends on the phone. I also talk to pretend friends on the phone and in the room. With all the above pretend places, the pretend characters come vibrantly to life and they pace the room with me, sing to me, sit by me on the bed. If I am pretend sick, they pretend worry, pretend threaten to call an ambulance.

None of them involve coaxing an old man twice a day into changing his panties, nor convincing a feisty cat it is far better to stay inside and have his dinner as opposed to spending the rainy night under a car. Yes, motels for birthdays and award shows.

Not this birthday/award show weekend. I have to be in town for this thing.

Birthday dawns, I delay getting out of bed. I hear him, stumbling around. A fog of unease swirls around me. Yeah, this is going to be bad for you, you should have gotten away. Lila had made noise about dinner, but Lila has been sick for days. She will cancel, of course, as she should. Panic starts to rise. At least you have kept the aide in for tonight to take care of him, thank God you didn't cancel her. Though when Lila cancels you will have nowhere to go and too late for a motel. This is going to be very very bad for you.

Darling, come on in, I am just finishing up these lines for tomorrow's shoot. What a long day today, yes? Toss me a banana from the tray, would you? We'll order food soon, yes? The others are coming over soon? We can all run lines over dinner. Let's get liquor in here. I'm running a bath, throw me that kimono, would you, with that bath foamy stuff. Never mind, don't start, you wish. Maybe later. You call for food and liquor for all of us and I'll leave the door open so we can still talk.

(From the bathtub)

You know how much I love Gary, right? I know you know. But I swear to God, I told him forty times, if he breaks during that scene, I will too, and we will never get through it. How many times did we reshoot that bitch today, 10? 12? The minute I get to how could you just leave me on the beach, blah blah, I'm looking at him

182

and he just starts to weep. Did you see that? Christ almighty. So, of course, I am weeping and can't get through it. Poor Ang, what a saint. How many re-takes was it? Was it 14? Really? Oh no, I'm sure not (falsely modest here), no, this won't be my year, please I won't even get a nom, how sweet of you to think so, though. Though I DO think the goddamn press department could get a little more aggressive about this sort of thing, but that's not why we do it, is it?

God love Gary, the best there is, really. Oh, don't be ridiculous, no he doesn't either, you're being stupid (gaily laugh here), he just gets like that when he's in a role. I did not, we never did. I don't know who told you that. Stupid. Did room service come? Can you bring in some champagne? No, you, can't stay in here. When will the others be here? I hope they are all ready to run a few scenes. Funny how Gary said he couldn't drop by tonight. Huh. I know he's not called tomorrow but, still.... Stop being that way. Goddamn him. Ok, I am getting out now. Oh, ha, you've worn me down, OK, quick before the others get here. Don't mention this to Gary.

Lila cancels. She is very sick. My throat starts to close up as panic starts to throttle.

Dad, let's go into the bathroom and get changed. No, we didn't just change, that was last night. (Again, again, again, again.) Changed, pilled, I sit him down for his lunch.

It's my birthday, I say.

Oh, he says. Really? How old are you?

59

Wow, you're old.

I laugh. Indeed, I am, but that means you are, too. He laughs.

Throat almost closed off entirely now, I wonder what to do with the rest of the day. I will get into the truck and drive, no destination, get near the water, that's all I want, to be near the water.

Lila messages me. Let's have lunch, let's get a manicure.

I laugh, (LOL), girl you go straight back to bed. No way, lunch and a manicure. No way. I'm fine, stay in bed.

She insists, she insists. She drags off her deathbed. She picks me up. We get our nails done. We have lunch. We gossip about boys.

She drops me back at the house late afternoon. The aide is already there, taking care of Dad for the evening. Pretend I'm not here, I say. You two carry on. I go to the back and message some friends. I speak on the phone with a couple. I get ready to go back out. Go out alone, to the pub, get a drink, talk to the ladies, have an early bite and then it will be over.

I take a birthday phone call at the bar. Lana says to me, it's your birthday? What are you doing later?

Oh, I'm seeing a bunch of bitches later, I toss out.

Oh, great, Lana says. She waits a beat, then asks, do you want cake?

Oh no, I answer, nonchalantly. (Please, those waiting bitches will have cake are you kidding?)

No, thanks Lana. I'm sure someone will have cake.

Hire Somebody Else

My hand shook over the submit button. It had been three

days to get this far. A long three-day weekend, plenty of time to get

those applications in. Plenty. But huh, gee, lookey-here, Netflix has

every single episode of Murder She Wrote. Every single one (I

think). Bemoaning the fact that I can't get Monk on Netflix, nor

Amazon Plus for that matter, I cast my eye to the capers of Murder

She Wrote. Yes, I am aware that MSW is geared to eighty-year olds

weaned on CBS, but it just might be the ticket over this long

weekend, embarrassing for me as it may be. I am pretty deep into

The Wire these days, but I have been sick with a bad cold and am

thinking about these job applications and I know I don't have the

head space for the Baltimore docks. I can, however, cram Jessica

Fletcher in there somewhere. I eye the applications, buried beneath a stack of bills. I had handily printed out the job descriptions and tossed them on the desk Friday afternoon. On Saturday morning, unable to meet their unblinking gaze, I moved them to the bottom of the bill pile. Let's recap, shall we? I would rather look at a pile of bills than these two job applications.

I had been temping for a bit at a local college. The opportunity had arisen to apply for one of two open permanent positions. I was waffling.

Why in God's name is it impossible to stream Mr. Monk? I poisoned-penned Amazon Plus. Yes, I do see all the options to buy all the seasons on DVD, but you need to understand I just want to stream Adrian Monk whenever I want to stream Adrian Monk. I am paying this monthly fee; I don't want to buy DVDs on top of that. Don't direct me to your excellent selection of other streaming videos (how excellent can it be, really) no Mr. Monk? I am going to have to re-think my membership, thank you and good day. I said good day sir.

Comfort-watching old detective series goes back awhile. I can always tell I am going through a real freak-out phase of life by what I am watching. In Los Angeles, in the 90s, it was Columbo. In New York City in the early 2000's, it was Monk. Now, here in the woods I have already gone through the Poirots on Netflix. Actually, Poirot was pushing it a bit. Hercule is a bit too intellectual and there needs to be a high camp factor to count as a comfort-watch. When I am well and fearless it is certainly The Wire, or any of the PBS Inspector Morse/Lewis series. When I am, er, not well and mewling it needs to be straight up formulaic, quirky-character, where's-my-afghan, just-fix-everything Lieutenant Columbo and Mr. Monk. In the mewling phase I can't even handle a Criminal Intent marathon, because, D'Onofrio. So, these days it will have to be Jessica Fletcher as I am betting the camp factor will be off the chain.

The new lawyer was a little less lawyerly than the previous lawyer, but not by much. I switched eldercare lawyers a couple of months ago because I was afraid of the first one. I never had to deal with a lawyer and he was fast, rushed. I doddered my daddy in, we signed powers of attorneys, and we talked wills. We talked what happens when I move to California, yes I am taking him with me. Do you want to go to California with her? Well yes I do, that will be alright, he says. That will be alright. What happens when we, I, sell the house and move to California? Does the will hold up? What happens then? Don't change the will, he has dementia, too late now. Do you want to go to California with her? Yes, that will be alright. No, I am not working here in Massachusetts, I have a job in California. I am taking him to California, far far away from here. Far away from here. Are you sure you want to go to California with her? Yes, that will be alright.

I tried to listen as the lawyer talked legalese loud and fast. I signed some stuff.

OK, so no Monk, it will have to be Jessica Fletcher. I eye the pile of bills and feel the Massachusetts job applications start to heave from below the pile.

I text Tommy in CA: Mary I am sitting here working on a pile of bills and wishing I could stream me some Mr. Monk. Instead, I got Murder She Wrote going with real D-listers as guest stars. I am thinking of you and Scoot. You marys would be howling.

Tommy: Oh mary, WE LOVE MURDER SHE WROTE! That busybody Jessica is gonna get herself shot though.

A month later, I went to work. I had been looking for a job for two years. The money situation was getting scary. My eighty-six-year-old father was the sole breadwinner (social security) until I wound my way through the state regulations of becoming his foster care provider. Still, neither income would be enough. He was getting too frail to make the trip to California. I am stuck here. I have to have independent income other than his meager social security and the foster care stipend as I weigh nursing home options.

The temp agency got me something at a local college. 9-5, close to the house, it wasn't bad really. It worked for some months, but underneath there was always an unease with leaving him alone during the day. I had aides in to check, along with the Meals on Wheels Lady, but still...

Me: Right? LOL. I could shoot her myself!

Tommy: Girl's up in everybody's business!

Working a full-time job, coming home, shopping, meal prep, pills, changing his clothes, bathing, uhh no. My aide and I called it the Three P's: Pills, Porridge and Panties. Exhausted, after I gave him his dinner, it was all I could do to crawl to my back room and flop down in front of the laptop.

Me: This eppy has that powerhouse Gabe Kaplan and Jeff Conaway in a dress. Poetry. Perfect to pay bills to.

Tommy: OMG!!! Where's Hal Linden and Judd Hirsch when u need them? Mary, what wouldn't I give to be there with u now?

This full-time thing is killing me, I say to my chiropractor. Who works full-time?? He asks if I am stretching, doing the exercises. No and No. Taking care of myself these days is out of the question.

Me: You can see Gabe did it from a mile away.

Tommy: My money was on Jeff.

Me: Jeff comic foil. And that superstar Genie Francis.

Tommy: Dame Genie Francis ADORES!!

Me: I know you do, my mary.

191

Five-ish months at the college and that temp assignment ended. The agency placed me at a new college in a temp-to-hire situation. I'd been warned about the new boss, he is difficult, it's an intense place, maybe it'll be different but I don't know I doubt it don't say we didn't warn you. Yes, it was intense, with long hours. It was further from my house than I wanted to travel. I didn't want to deal with the special events and I don't care about homecoming weekend and trustees coming in.

Dad you didn't eat your lunch today? Did you not see it on the table? You have to eat when they leave it for you, I can't be here during the day because I am working at this job where I don't care about their special events and weird personalities and trustees coming in and homecoming weekends. Homecoming. Homecoming. Coming Home. If you don't eat your lunch I can't leave you alone and I can't work. Or we have to talk about the nursing home again and you won't be able to live at home. I am trying to keep you safe at home, that is why we are talking about this now. I will visit you and then come back home but you will have to stay there where the nurses can watch you do you understand what's happening?

Me: OK, this eppy is Hurray for Homicide. John Saxon, Ron Palillo, Lyle Waggoner. It is a wonder when I look up I can see stars in the sky at all. They all seem to have fallen on a Murder She Wrote set.

Tommy: Waggoner's goin' down and Saxon did it. Just guessin'.

Me: My money is on Palillo. And Jessica is always running out to meet snitches at 9 or 10PM. She's gonna get her ass shot off.

Tommy: LOL, Jessica's on thin ice.

The college is moving fast to fill this temp position. They ask me if I am throwing my hat in the ring. I guess so, I think to myself. (Ughh, difficult personalities, special events, trustees coming to town, ughhh.) I guess I will, yeah. I dig the job applications from underneath the pile of bills.

Me: James Coco just got knocked off and Kristoffer Tabori is looking good for it.

Tommy: LOVES. And I bet that nosy old bat is asking questions and taking names.

Me: Yes, she is. Tabori is going to shoot her ass off. Uhh, let's meet at 10PM in a deserted amusement park and hope Kristoffer Tabori doesn't shoot our asses off. Real smart, Jessica

Tommy: That bitch is going down.

I fill out the applications. I, hands shaking, hit submit. At work, they tell me they have my application. They tell me they will schedule an interview for me. OK, I say. OK.

When it is quiet in the office, when they are all out greeting trustees and meeting about how to make the events special, I hear the clock tick. The clock on the wall ticks loudly and calmly. It ticks like the one in my grandmother's, my father's mother's, parlor in Maine. It ticks like I heard it tick that summer 40 years ago.

Oh well, Grandma knows, she says.

Do you, Grandma? Do you know the hell she has created? Daddy is never home anymore, he can't stand it. It's just me and

Larry with her. I can't stand it I can't stand it I can't stand it. My stomach hurts all the time now. Silence. The clock ticks, tick tock, tick tock. Grandma knows, she says. We will ask if you can stay an extra week up here in Maine. Tick. You will not have to go back to that house for an extra week. Tock. Won't we have fun? Tick. Grandma will teach you to sew that pant-suit and we will cook. Tock. Let's sit in the parlor and have tea and some pie. Tick Tock.

The interview is tomorrow. Tick tock. I go back to that house every day from this job. Every day when I get back something new is happening. An uneaten, non-understood lunch (Dad, if they leave it on the table for you, you HAVE to eat it), more poopy, endless poopy. Spilled coffee.

Me: Belinda Montgomery, Vicki Lawrence, Lynda Day George, Jo Anne Worley and Leslie Nielson. Star studded episode, my mary.

Tommy: LOVES this lineup. Jessica needs to watch her back around Ms. Jo Anne Worley.

Me: Indeed, not as far as we can throw her, that Ms. Worley.

Interview day. I don't interview well, unsurprisingly. The old familiar, Tell us why you want to work here, I am too exhausted to even fake well. I don't actually. I never really did. The agency sent me. I don't care about any of this and homecoming and the special events. There was a time in my life when I DID care about those things, believe me (well, I sorta cared), but not now.

I prettied it up. I slung some bullshit about America's youth and the future of the kids, but I do believe they saw through that. That belief was confirmed a few days later as I was brought in to my supervisor's office and she almost tearfully told me I wasn't a finalist. They hired somebody else.

Uh huh. I said. OK. They asked if I wanted to stay on while my replacement was on-boarded. The prospect of staying in a job that I didn't get, while actually doing the job that I didn't get, didn't appeal. I gave a weeks' notice.

Tommy: We always try to guess who's throwing it to Jessica. At our house, she is getting some every episode. Usually it's William Windom.

Me: I noticed that, too! There is usually an associate that we think is throwing it to her. Last eppy it was Jerry Orbach. She gets it more in one season than I ever got in my life.

Tommy: Our girl is busy.

During interview week, the unusual activity at home had increased. I caught him playing with the stove. Testing it to see if it works, he says. I caught him emptying a shit-bucket in the tub. Oh, well, this is what I always do, he says.

No, this is not what we always do. At night it's worse.

I hear a thumping on the wall, then a crash, I roll over. No, it's not happening, maybe I dreamed it. I shoosh the cat off the bed.

The other one, alert, slides in, gets up on the bed. Usually they fight but not tonight, no not tonight.

I think I hear a voice. I roll back over. I look at the clock, 3AM. Did I just hear a voice?

I close my eyes. I hear a louder voice. I hear more thumping on the wall. The other cat jumps back on the bed. They walk upwards towards my head. One of them yowls, the talker. What, I say, what now?

He yowls back, you better get up and see, get up and see. It's happening, the beginning of the end is happening are you just going to lie there? The end is nigh, it's coming, it's all changing now in these last ten minutes. You need to witness. You won't be able to stop this now that this is changing fast like this, but you should at least get up and see it. You won't be able to help him much now but you should get up and see, get up and see. And while you are getting up and seeing, we're hungry. Feed us.

I get up. The voice is louder, though not in distress. Another thump. I stop at the edge of the door.

California fades.

I give the Of Mice and Men speech to myself and the cats. Tell us about the rabbits again, George. We'll have a garden and a pen for the rabbits and we'll grow our own food and it'll be sunny all the time.

Me: God, Tommy, I can't work while he is like this, it's too dangerous at home, and I can't get him to California. I have to figure out what to do.

Next-to-last day my supervisor hands me a bunch of resumes. These are the No's. Can you shred them please? I see mine. I shred it first.

But Jessica is definitely doing William Windom.

Checking the Manual

Chop Suey - onions, hamburger, a large can of tomatoes.
Pasta. No garlic. I often debated, garlic or not. It looks like it wants
garlic. But no, no garlic. Grandma and Dad never used garlic. (Oh
you fancy New Yorkers and your garlic, no, us plain folks don't fuss
with any garlic.) The type of pasta is important, too. Not spaghetti,
because then... well, it's spaghetti with meat sauce. I once tried to
fob off I was making Bolognese to a friend and got schooled. Dear,
is there veal? Are there carrots and celery? Did you simmer for
forty-two hours? Uhh, no. Then, dear, you're making spaghetti with
meat sauce. Oh. (The culinary circle of disdain comes back around
to me.)

The chop suey pasta was elbow macaroni. Not penne, not the little corkscrew things, had to be elbow. Now chop suey dates back well before the infinite varieties of pasta on the market now. There was probably only the two kinds then, anyway, elbow and spaghetti.

Today was the day, I could tell. I knew. Well, the last two days have been Today Was The Day, sitting vigil. I scooted into work that Monday, since the past two days weren't The Day, I rolled the dice and thought I would get a little work done, maybe Today's The Day would be a little later in the afternoon. The office was ten minutes away from the nursing home, I can get there fast. We worked a bit, maybe two hours, before the call came. He's slipping. Ok I will be right there. The chaplain called next, 5 minutes later.

OK, let's check the manual, I say to my sister-in-law. The nice hospice lady gave me a pamphlet after I rushed to the bedside that morning. How to Tell When Your Loved One is Catching the Last Train Out, or something like that. When this happens that is happening, along those lines.

Cindy hands me the manual.

After the call from the chaplain, my friends in the office gathered around me. Oh Betty, they say.

Yeah, I have to go. My friends enveloped me. A hug for papa on his way out. This afternoon will end my long exile in western Massachusetts. The exile began when I got the call from the Massachusetts social services lady: What the hell is the matter with you, your father is wandering around, can't figure out the checkbook, is dangerous around the stove and can't remember what he had for lunch. You need to come right now.

Now, four years later as I flip through the manual, I hold my father's hand and talk him through it. The nice nursing home folks have closed off our part of the room and brought in a trolley for the vigil. Juice, crackers, coffee. Cindy hands me coffee. You need to eat, she says. I'm going for food.

Grab me a charger, I ask, the cell is dying and everyone and their mother is checking in. I say that annoyedly, as if it were SO much trouble to talk and text folks who are asking about my father. What the fuck is wrong with me?

Daddy, this will be OK. I'm right here and we are together for a little while longer. Cindy is coming back and we'll have a little bite together, isn't that nice? I know I know you always loved Cindy

she knows that let me fix that pillow are you warm enough that aide

you like, what's his name Chris, Casey? He brought some coffee

and juice and peanut butter and jelly sandwiches but Cindy and I

wanted real food so she skedaddled out to get us something to eat

can you smell the coffee Daddy I'm going to fix you a cup.

Cindy comes back with food and a charger. We set up food

around my father's bed.

Daddy, Cindy is back and she's here for dinner. Isn't that

nice we have some company over. Look, Daddy, I have Special

Victims Unit on, yes, it's still on it's been on all day. One of those

marathons, ha! Maybe we'll see my episode, wouldn't that be fun?

OK Dad, I'm going to make us supper soon. Do you want chop

suey? Yeah, I'll make that. Remind me again, do I chop the onions

first? That rough chop, right? Yeah, I'll get that going soon. We

will have supper soon, you, me and Cindy. It's been awhile since we

all had supper together, nice, huh?

Dad starts, and the breathing changes, starts to hitch. Cindy

and I look at each other in alarm as I reach for the manual.

Breathing will slow and may become erratic.

Oh, OK.

Yep, everything is OK, Dad. You're doing just great. Dinner is almost ready, can you smell the chop suey simmering? And the coffee, wait, I'll get you another cup.

After awhile, Cindy leaves.

It's just my father and I, as it always was. Around 5PM, I quietly talk him out.

I sit with him for a long time. I listen to the nursing home bustle outside the room. It's dinner time for the residents. I look out the window. There is a robin on the lawn.

On November 3rd, 2017 I gave the eulogy at my father's memorial

service.

Here is part of it.

My father was a quiet, simple man. If he ever met you, he liked you. People liked him. Despite the turmoil around where and how he was living, he kept his kindness and gentleness. He wasn't one for emotion. On one of my very rare trips back here, I can't remember if he said it to me directly, or said to someone in my presence, but it was, It doesn't matter where she is, or if we see each other again or not, Cathy and I understand each other. I never forgot that and it comforted me when we didn't see each other over the years, it felt like he travelled with me.

I'll tell just the one story that symbolizes who my father was, the unexpected soul and spirit of him. I've told the Wedding Story before to a few of you, I posted it last night on Facebook with one of the wedding pictures and it got around pretty fast.

On my wedding day in New York City, Daddy and I were sitting in the priest's anti-chamber next to the main part of the church. The side door opened onto 177th St. A beautiful September day, the sun shone into the dark room. We could hear the guests entering the church. My father leaned over to me and said quietly and kindly, We could just slip out the door here and walk down 177th and get a cup of coffee at that diner. You don't have to do this.

I looked at him. He meant it. No, Dad. I'm OK. This will be OK.

Alright, dear, he said.

I picture in my mind's eye to this day my father and I strolling down the street and wrapping this doozy of a dress around one of those red counter stools with a cup of joe in front us.

With no disrespect to the-husband-to-be (God, can you imagine being married to me?), I should have taken Dad up on the offer.

That's the kind of dad he was.

So, Daddy, next time I see you, we will take that walk down 177th St on a beautiful September day, me in that long, foofey dress and that what was I thinking veil and have coffee in that diner.

And if, by some chance, we don't see each other for a very long time again, it doesn't matter where you are, yes, we always understood each other.

Thank you all for coming.

And That's Our Time

Everything is dying all at once, I say to Lila. The car, the house, the closing, the job. Why all at once? It's not fair. I wanted to let go on my own time. Rage against the dying of the light and all that bullshit. I need more time, I need more time.

Drunker than I usually **want** to be, I teeter up the slippery outside stairs. A lonesome cold rain was coming down hard, the clouds blocking the moon. In the dark, I clutched the wooden railing, dragged my hand to hoist myself up, and got a splinter. Fuck. I stop on the stairs. Fuck, this will really hurt. I lumber up, switching hands to the other railing to continue the hoisting. Before I get to the top, my hand is already throbbing. Hoist up one stair, then stop to wonder if I have a lighter. Hoist up another stair, I wonder if I have a needle. By the time I had hoisted to, and slipped, on the top landing, I was wondering if I had cotton balls and hydrogen peroxide. Shaking the rain out of my hair, I slide open the glass door. The cat, forever waiting, triumphantly escapes into the cold, wet black. I drop my shopping bags, full of food I will never eat, and come back out on the rickety ledge. I plaintively call for the cat. Come Back, Little Sheba, Come Back. Yes, we are that pathetic tonight. I might as well be Shirley Booth in a ratty housecoat, woefully standing in the rain. And now I'm Shirley Booth in a ratty housecoat, woefully standing in the rain with a goddamn splinter. I shuffle back inside, pulling the glass door shut.

You're on your own tonight, bub, I say to the closed door. Try not to decimate the baby bunny population in the yard. Baby Bunnies! He's out again! Run and try to save your little bunny asses!

I shake off my sweater, along with the guilt of a potential bunny massacre, turn on the dim lamp by the bed, and inspect the damage to my hand.

It's a splinter, for Christ's sake, how much "damage" can there be? I'm already over-dramatizing the situation. I'm already over-worrying about the escaped cat. I'm already over-drama-queening the house was falling down around me, that I was alone, everyone was dead, I should be sleeping in the car, I have no emergency contact, what if this splinter kills me? What then??? Do I have enough life insurance if this splinter kills me and poor Lila has to deal with funeral expenses? Who's going to call for that fucking cat?

Shake this shit off right now, sister and deal with the splinter.

Who the hell gets splinters anymore? Maybe when I was ten. I had a few splinters when I was ten. I'm now 140. You don't get splinters when you are 140. But a splinter I had. When I was ten, the splinter surgery was an exact and easy medical procedure for my parents. Well, for my father actually. He pulled out a silver Zippo lighter, that old-timey kind with a flint. He needed a needle. Sometimes my **usually** unconscious mother was **semi**-conscious and **somewhat** helpful in the needle department. Here, Roger, it's in the sewing can, and she would lift her head, wave vaguely at the old blue and gold Maxwell House coffee can, and drop back into herself.

Thanks, Ma, helpful. He would cross the room and grab the can. He'd fish out a needle, flip open the Zippo, lighter fluid smell swirling around me, temporarily distracting me with the smell of outboard motors on the lake. Wait, let me get the hydrogen peroxide, he'd say. Where is the peroxide? he'd ask her. She pulled up from her chest, cocked her head, and looked at us uncomprehendingly. Where. Is. The. Hydrogen. Peroxide? he'd say, louder, irritated. You could see a flicker of light behind her eyes. She waved towards the bathroom and dropped back down.

He got up, went to the bathroom and came back with the peroxide and a bag of cotton balls.

Now, now, he would say, this will only take a minute. I can see the splinter, it's right there, very close to the surface. This won't hurt at all, it will only be a minute. I turned my terrified face away from my mother, relieved to be back in the normal routine of splinter surgery.

There, there, he'd say. He snapped the wheel - igniter thing on the Zippo, cauterized the needle and carefully wiped it down with the cotton ball and peroxide. It was easy and quick. He deftly pierced my finger and ran the needle under the wood, slipping it out in one movement.

Thanks, Daddy!

That's OK, go find your brother, I'll make supper for the three of us. Chop suey?

Fuck, I stopped smoking. I don't have a lighter. I don't have a needle. I have to get a sewing kit, I have to sew buttons on shit. For that matter, I don't have hydrogen peroxide. I DO have cotton balls.

Without the necessary medical equipment, I compromise. I take a paper clip and untwist it. Will this do? I'm doubtful. It's not sharp enough and it's probably filthy. I can't cauterize or sterilize. Well, you have to try. I get up, slide open the door, totter onto the balcony and into the storm and call for the cat. Sheba, Sheba!! No sign of him and it's too Shirley Booth for me. Fuck him, come back in the morning, fucker.

I sit on the bed and start the incision. No, the paper clip isn't going to work, I can see the splinter, but it seems to be in pretty deep. What if I poison myself? What if I get sepsis from this filthy paper clip? I dig deeper. No luck. Now I can't see it at all. Jesus Christ, what if I have pushed it into my bloodstream. Then you are really fucked, little wood chips will flow through your veins. I dig deeper. I pull back a flap of skin. I start to bleed. No, I will win this, Splinter, you will lose this war. I dig deeper, pull back another flap of skin and bleed harder. I stop myself here. Jesus Christ, Cathy. Is this the metaphor for this time in your life? Tear your own flesh apart? Do you really need to rip the skin off your body to punish yourself for not being up to the task? Maybe I should take the flesh-ripping thing down a notch.

I put down the clip and dab my hand with a dry cotton ball. The splinter still can't be seen. Maybe it's gone, washed away by blood. Maybe it's flowing through my bloodstream, making little baby woodchips.

I lie down and listen to the rain. Baby bunny-less, Cheddar is waiting outside in the morning.

The car was starting to smoke. These days I smelled oil and something was dripping. I never checked under the car to see where it was dripping from. I don't want to know where it is dripping from, or even if it really WAS dripping. Maybe it's not dripping, maybe I have that wrong. Sure, I must have that wrong. When it started to make funny noises, I worried more. Though I didn't worry enough to look under the bottom, or hood, or wherever you're supposed to look. I need to call Don, the mechanic. I will next week.

This car needs to hold out until the house is sold and I will have the extra money then to buy a new one.

Jack the realtor calls, the closing is pushed back another month. *NO, MOTHERFUCKER, YOU TELL THEM NO. That will make it the fourth time since the beginning of the year. I can't hold on another month, I couldn't hold on another month when you told me the last time the closing was being pushed. I can't hold on.* I didn't really call him a motherfucker. He's a good, patient boy who has been my realtor the whole time. Yes, I wanted to dump him on occasion, I don't need a good, nice, patient boy as a realtor, I need a motherfucker, a shark, an aggressive bitch. *The hellhole should have been dumped last year, why can't you push these prospects harder, motherfucker?* I said none of those things to Jack, but I did say, you know I'm through with this, right? You know I'm at the end? You know it's not fair to me? Can't you call them and say, hey, that's not fair to her?

Oh yes, I will let them know. I will certainly tell them. But there's not much we can do. Then he launched into the boring details why. The bank this and that, they didn't get the paperwork in on time. *Why the fuck not, motherfucker?* We were missing a signature, the paperwork had to be sent back, oh wait, I think maybe they changed banks, another lender had to be brought in to verify the first estimate and now we need a separate estimate. I listened, tears springing to my eyes. I contemplated crawling under my desk and taking a little nappie. I squeaked OK then, but you tell them this is the last time, right? I'm at the end. I don't think I can hold out, nothing else can go wrong.

The car was now lurching, not keeping herself in gear. Much like her mommy. It would glide down some hills, but would be unable to climb up hills. On the way to work, I began to figure out how to get a running start to make the hills. No, I can't take it in yet. With the new closing date, she only has to last two more weeks, two more weeks. We can hang on for two weeks, sure we can.

There was a trip to Connecticut coming up. That trip is about 150 miles. Sure, we will make that. It's not too bad if I give her a running start to get up the hills. I've learned to do that, I've mastered that technique.

The ink froze in the pen as the temperature dropped in the house. It was too cold to write. The cats, who could normally take me or leave, crawled in bed with me. The pipes had frozen again this winter. The ancient house wouldn't see another winter. For that matter, neither would the cats or myself if I didn't figure this shit out right now. I had gotten estimates from the insurance company. It takes forever, I was behind on all the utility bills by now. Another assessor had to come by the house and inspect something I-don't-even-know-what outside. Meanwhile, still no heat while this got sorted. Two weeks later the insurance company issued a check to me. I paid off the fuel people, who fixed the pipes, and as I was behind on the fuel bills proper, paid that balance too. Unfortunately, I couldn't pay the electricity bill, which was somehow tied into how the heater thing worked, so I was still fucked. The electricity bills, along with the propane bills I was racking up using portable heaters, were finally crashing me.

I call Jack. Are we on target to close in two weeks? Cause I'm crashing here. I want to keep this as nice as I can for the new folks. I think maybe I lied as to the extent of how far I was crashing, lest Jack would think less of me.

I did tell Lila. I'm crashing, I said, matter- of-factly. Lila tells me, this is only temporary, Betty. This will all work out once the house is sold. The house is dying, Lila. I can't turn the heat on, I can't cook or light the stove anymore.

The car didn't make it to Connecticut. It stalled in back-to-back traffic on that hill right after The Tunnel of Heroes on the Merritt. Two kindly gentlemen pulled over and started walking towards me. Numb to it all now, I shut the car off, then turned her back on. Two more weeks, two more weeks. She started back up and I discovered I could bring her back to life by only driving in low gear.

Claire says to me, hey I have an idea. I'll loan you $5000 and we never speak of it again, and then you apply for a car loan at the credit union and tell them you have $5000 for a down payment. I laugh gaily and say, oh no I couldn't possibly, thanks so much. But I'm not a LOSER. You don't think I'm a LOSER do you, does everybody think I'm a LOSER???? Ha ha, how funny, Claire but aren't you the sweetest? No, I'm fine, really.

Turns out, you can only drive a car in low gear for so long. She was making angrier and angrier noises every time I fired her up and shifted to low. I know you're tired, I would say, I know. We're all tired here. Please, please hang on for two more weeks. No, she snapped back one cold March day. No, I won't hang on for one more mile, she howled and ka-thunked. I managed to get her over to the side, one mile from the freezing, dying house.

Claire asked if she could loan me some money again. No, I love you but no thanks. I'll figure it out.

I've been riding my luck, too long, Lila. Living off these credit cards, while I was taking care of the old man, staying in a crappy paying job in a college about to close. It's all come back to haunt me. Lila and I had a running joke, she, a physical therapist, would sign off her sessions with particularly chatty clients by saying "And that's our time." Ahh, that's smart. A lovely way to put it, not dismissive, but a polite way of saying "We're done now, we all need to move on." Until the next session, chapter.

Lila, the house, the car, the college, all of western Massachusetts is saying "And that's our time, Cathy."

What do I do now, what do I do now? This can't be "And that's our time, Cathy." It's NOT our time quite yet. I am SO close to the finish line in western Massachusetts: Dead Daddy, this shithole house. All wrapped up in two glorious weeks and then I get to be me, alone, figuring out where and what I want to be.

With Claire's $5K in my account, I call the loan officer about my application. The Irish loan officer was skeptical. She mentions my credit score is pretty low. Ya think? I tell her a little bit of my story. I sense I am beneath her. I know, I acknowledge, it doesn't look very good. BUT only for two weeks and I can pay it back. And I have a down payment!! Well, she says, your credit score.... I know, lately my credit score has dropped faster than my panties at a Bon Jovi concert. She asks me if I have another loan out. Yes, I do, Loan Betty. How are you going to pay that back? Well, in now two weeks... I start to mewl. I don't finish mewling before she asks me and how do you have the down payment? Well, you see, Loan Betty, it turns out that I am SUCH A LOSER, and my friend Claire smartly recognized that I am the biggest LOSER on the planet and she kindly loaned me the $5 thousand. If I put the phone down in Amherst, I could have heard the sigh over the wind from Hadley. And JUST how are you GOING to pay THAT one back? I'm silent, I don't even try.

Oh shoot, Loan Betty, I almost forgot, you are right! I am a worthless piece of shit. How could I forget that? You know what would have been easier for us all, why didn't I drive that car into a tree while I had the chance, oh oopsie, no go with that, I can't get the car over 30 in low gear.

I almost tell HER don't give me the loan.

Claire's five thousand bridges a cheap used car and getting the utilities back on. Getting the utilities back on for the new owners. Sold. The cats start speaking to me again.

Moving day. Claire and her husband help me pack the few things I want. I don't want much.

And that's our time, dead family. On to my solo time. Time that, for right now, doesn't involve thinking about you anymore.

Go back to New York, he said, my first week back home.

Don't you think I want to, old man? I was screaming. I'm fucked here. You have fucked me. My life is fucking over. This is the end for me.

I can live alone. I've lived alone for years.

No, you can't old man. The fucking social workers called me in New York. The fucking state of Massa- fucking- chusetts fucking called me. At fucking work.

She was mean, that social worker, loud, brassy. She brayed into the phone. Do you know your father is wandering around the stores? He is leaving open flames on, he isn't paying any bills, there are mice all over the place, he isn't keeping his medical appointments, we don't know if he is eating.

I pictured what this woman looked like. I saw her office. It was dingy and dusty and there were three outdated calendars on her desk, a pencil on the floor, that institutional green. Probably a picture of the governor on the wall. Her message light was blinking that orange red on the phone. There were stacks of manila files in front of her, all with handwritten titles in pencil. Too busy or too disorganized or no budget for a label maker, she handwrote the titles. She herself was impeccably dressed. A dark navy suit on. She was middle aged and heavily made-up, her skin too bronzed, the shade veered into orange. She wore blue eyeshadow, a baby blue, and a lot of it, that didn't match the navy suit. The jewelry was clunky and gold. A big necklace was around her neck, large gold interconnected circles, with big gold heavy loops for earrings. Her lipstick was fire engine-red and the lipstick was all around her mouth and below and above her lip line. A lipstick stained coffee cup was to her right. The decaf in the pot on the back file cabinet was almost burnt down.

Now she was yelling at me. Who's taking care of him? Who is monitoring this situation? Is there any family there, because this is totally unacceptable.

I sputter something... well my brother recently died and I was under the impression my sister-in-law and the grandkids were checking in every now and then... I trailed off... shock froze my throat.

Well, you need to make arrangements or re-locate back yourself. He absolutely cannot live alone, he is a danger to himself. Is he driving still? Sputter sputter, yes, I think so.

You don't know???? She was yelling louder. You need to come back right away. He needs to see a doctor right away.

You can't live alone, don't you get it? If I leave, you go into a fucking nursing home old man, the fucking state actually takes you, do you get that? So, no, I can't go back to New York.

I'm fine here alone.

No, Daddy, you're not fine. You're not fine. None of this is fine, for either of us. But we have to make this work. We have to find a way.

I sit on the couch, suddenly tired.

I look over at him, he in his easy chair, the television on.

We look at each other.

I start to laugh. Fuck, huh, Daddy?

He laughs, fuck is right.

What do you want for supper, Daddy? Do you want me to make you some chop suey? We have cottage cheese and pickles. Good, huh?

Oh yes, dear, that will be good.

Do you want me to make you some coffee, or do you want a beer?

Oh, maybe a beer.

Yes, good idea, a beer I think. I'll bring it to you.

Friends come over to help me with the actual move. A lot of friends, four or five. As we pull out, I take a last look at the old house. I'm moving to a room that is up a large set of stairs. Due to limited mobility, I hear Gracie tell the others not to let me carry stuff up the stairs. They bring all the stuff up, I just point where it goes.

The cats go last.

Acknowledgements

LOVE and THANKS to my editors and cheerleaders and friends at the Grapeville Grille who got both Dad and I through.

Made in the USA
Middletown, DE
11 December 2019